WHAT WORKS

and doesn't, with At Risk Students

WHAT WORKS
and dosen't, with At Risk Students

Jan Glaes

BKS Publishing
Mill Creek, Washington
(425) 745-3029

Published in the United States by, BKS, a division of Professional Development Institute.

Distributed by Professional Development Institute, Mill Creek, Washington.

ISBN: 0-9656713

Dedication

This book is dedicated to all those who work in public schools, especially the children.

It is offered with the hope that it will help to create schools where all students can succeed.

Contents

Acknowledgments

I would like to thank Patricia Reeves, Superintendent of Vicksburg Community Schools, for her support in this endeavor. Her vision of what education could be is an inspiration to those who know her.

I would also like to thank Bill Blokker for his dedication, persistence, supportand creativity in bringing this work to completion.

Thanks go also to Sue Blokker for proofing, organizing, keeping track of things and I am sure so much more.

Lastly, I want to thank my husband, Charles, for his ability to listen, critique, suggest, care for the family, and love and support me always.

Author's Note

The intent of this document is to present a comprehensive summary of the research on the topic of at-risk students and to enable educators to be more effective in the teaching process. In order to do this, the author has summarized and paraphrased large numbers of research documents, books, articles, and papers. The author makes no claims of ownership on any of these findings or works.

Whenever possible, studies which employed meta-analysis methods were used in this literature review in order to determine the effectiveness of the various strategies. Homes (1989) gives an excellent description of this method as well as its benefits:

> Meta-analysis is a relatively recent and sophisticated method for integrating the findings of multiple research studies. It has several important features that recommend it over traditional narrative reviews. First, meta-analytic summaries are more comprehensible to the reader than lengthy recounting of each individual study methods and results. Second, the quantification of effects is based on the actual difference between treated and control groups averaged across studies rather than tests of statistical significance. Traditional vote counting methods that tally important differences can alternately obscure or exaggerate practically important differences because of their dependence on sample size. Finally, meta-analysis permits systematic examination of study attributes that might influence study results. In the case of retention research, for example, do studies where promoted and retained children are well matched on initial characteristics lead to the same conclusions as studies with poorer controls? Although there is

> always more to be learned from future research, these features of meta-analysis enable a definitive statement about what research says on a topic (16).

When researchers use the common scale of Effect Size, or ES, they are able to carry out sophisticated analysis of results from a variety of different studies. ES most often refers to the number of standard deviation units that separates outcome scores of experimental and control groups. The average score of the control group is subtracted from the average score of the experimental group, and the remainder is then divided by the standard deviation of the measure.

What is an At-Risk Student?

As the at-risk population drops out of school or graduates with substandard skills, what is the cost to society when students become citizens who are not prepared to become productive workers? And, more importantly, what is the cost to these students — the cost of lost self-esteem and of living with a sense of hopelessness about their abilities and their future? Districts that successfully educate their at-risk population gain a great deal in terms of productive time use; financial considerations; contributions to society and the development of productive; confidant individuals. This is why it is both important and beneficial for school districts to take a long, hard look at their at-risk population. If asked, classroom teachers will attest to the fact that they spend an inordinate amount of time working with and assisting a small number of these students each year in their classrooms, often with less than satisfying results. It is also difficult to estimate the financial cost to districts when at-risk students need the services of special education classrooms, Chapter I teachers, in-house suspension programs, and other alternative education methods.

Why worry about the at-risk students?

What is an at-risk student ?

Although "at-risk" has become a commonly used term in educational research today, its meaning is anything but clear. No universally accepted definition has been agreed upon by scholars. The term "high-risk students" first appeared in the Educational Resources Information Center's (ERIC) Thesaurus of ERIC Descriptors in 1980. As "students, with normal intelligence, whose academic background or prior performance may cause them to be perceived as candidates for future academic failure or early withdrawal" (p. 116). Although prior to 1980 the database used terms such as "disadvantaged students" and "underachievement," the term "high-risk" indicates the idea of a student's propensity towards or probability of underachievement. For the purposes of this document, the following definition for an at-risk student will be used:

> ***Someone who is unlikely to graduate on schedule with both the skills and self-esteem necessary to exercise meaningful options in the areas of work, leisure, culture, civic affairs, inter/intra personal relationships* (Sagor, 1993, p. 4).**

Describing this diverse student population is a difficult task. In the 1989 AASA Critical Issues Report, Students At-Risk: Problems and Solutions, Brodinsky & Keough state the following:

> In reality, there can be no single, working definition of an at-risk student because the definition must vary from community to community, from school to school and, very possibly, from year to year. The basis of a definition, as well as the basis of a district's program for identifying students at-risk, then becomes a list of the characteristics of the potential drop out (p. 39-40).

The following characteristics, compiled from at-risk research and grouped into four categories by Wells (1990), attempt to describe students who are likely to fall short of our intended educational outcomes — in other words, students who are "at-risk." These characteristics, listed in no particular order, include:

Family Related Characteristics

1. Low socioeconomic status (SES) (Peng & Tahai, 1983; Swanson, 1991)
2. Low educational achievement and occupational attainment level of parents (Rumberger, 1983; Steinberg, Blinde & Chan, 1982; Bachman, 1971)
3. Large families (Rumberger, 1983; Steinberg, Blinde & Chan, 1982; Bachman, 1971)
4. Weak family cohesiveness or single-parent family (Rumberger, 1983; Steinberg, Blinde & Chan, 1982; Bachman, 1971)

5. Lack of learning materials and opportunities in the home (Rumberger, 1983; Steinberg, Blinde & Chan, 1982; Bachman, 1971)
6. Child abuse and neglect (Sartain, 1989)
7. Loss of one or both parents (Sartain, 1989)
8. Lack of social-emotional support from family (Sartain, 1989)
9. Excessively stressful home environment (Brodinsky & Keough, 1989)
10. Poor communication between home and school (California State DOE, 1986)
11. Racial or ethnic minority (California State DOE, 1986)

12. Non-English speaking home (California State DOE, 1986)
13. Lack of adequate adult supervision — students left unsupervised for long periods of time (Muller, 1991a)
14. Frequent family moves (California State DOE)
15. Changing schools (California State DOE)
16. Inadequate food and poor nutrition resulting in a lack of energy for study and school work (Brodinsky & Keough, 1989)
17. Damage to dignity and self-esteem when impoverished student compares him or herself to others (Brodinsky & Keough, 1989)
18. Negative attitude of parents towards education, schools, and teachers (Brodinsky & Keough, 1989)
19. Parental reliance on television to "entertain" children (Brodinsky & Keough, 1989)
20. Lack of orderliness and discipline at home leading to student tardiness, absenteeism, and truancy (Brodinsky & Keough, 1989)
21. Drug and alcohol abuse by parents (Brodinsky & Keough, 1989)
22. Absence of good role models,either male or female, in home (Brodinsky & Keough, 1989).

School Related Characteristics

1. Poor academic achievement characterized by
   a. low achievement scores (San Diego, 1985)
   b. high retention rates (LAUSD, 1985)
   c. two or more years behind in reading or math (Weber, 1983)

d. basic skills well below average for grade level (Weber, 1983)
e. failure in one or more schools (Wisconsin, 1981; California, 1986).

2. Behavior problems at school which are visible since elementary school characterized by
   a. absenteeism (Wehlage & Rutter, 1986)
   b. truancy (Wehlage & Rutter, 1986)
   c. discipline problems (Wehlage & Rutter, 1986)
   d. feelings of alienation from schools, teachers, peers, home, neighborhoods, and/or society in general (LAUSD, 1985)
   e. tendency to perceive little interest, caring, or acceptance on the part of teachers (LAUSD, 1985)
   f. resentful feelings towards authority and feelings that the discipline system is unfair and ineffective (Wehlage & Rutter, 1986).

3. Organizational influences characterized by
   a. inflexible schools and school systems, especially "graded schools" where all students are expected to learn and retain information at the same pace or be left behind (Cuban, 1989)
   b. schools with inadequate teaching staffs and materials, as well as poor facilities (Fine, 1986)
   c. negative school environment or school climate including the lack of:
      - positive, cooperative relationships between and among students, staff, parents, and administrators;
      - adequate discipline procedures and/or policies;
      - alternative schools/programs to meet the needs of at-risk groups;
      - collaborative teamwork among school and community;
      - respect by teachers, who treat students as children with no responsibilities (Education Week, 1986; Stern, 1986);
   d. teacher preconceptions of at-risk students and their families (Richardson et al., 1989)
   e. course offerings inappropriate for students with low academic achievement (Brodinski & Keough, 1989)

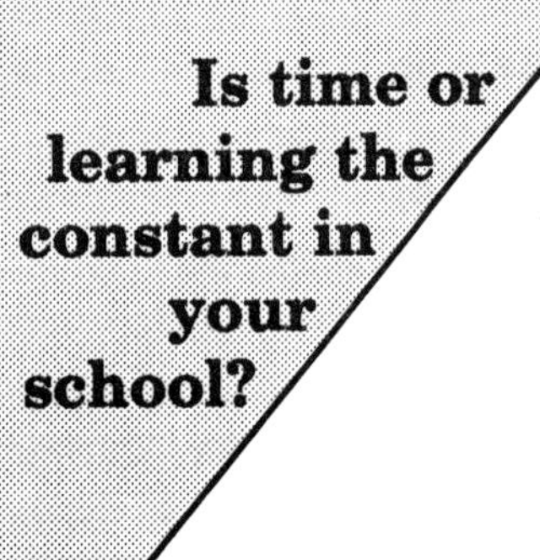

f. teaching style ineffective for at-risk students (Brodinski & Keough, 1989)
g. traditional emphasis on memorization and recitation, along with unnecessary verbalism(Brodinski & Keough, 1989).
h. lack of adequate counseling and school services for at-risk students (Brodinski & Keough, 1989)
i. excessive testing and faulty interpretation of test results (Brodinski & Keough, 1989)
j. disproportionate use of detention, suspension, and expulsion with at-risk students (Brodinski & Keough, 1989)
k. inadequate opportunities for extra-curricular activities to meet the needs of students who work (Brodinski & Keough, 1989)
l. rejection of low academic achievers by their more able peers (Brodinski & Keough, 1989)
m. failure of at-risk students to find meaningful experiences in school (Brodinski & Keough, 1989)

Student related characteristics

1. Low self-esteem (Swanson, 1991; Lehr & Harris, 1988; Rumberger, 1986)
2. Feelings of having little or no control over their lives (Rumberger, 1986)
3. Low educational and occupational aspirations (Ekstrom et al., 1986)
4. Immaturity (California, 1986)
5. Frequent health problems (California, 1986; Lehr & Harris, 1988)
6. Drug and alcohol abuse (California, 1986)
7. Pregnancy (California, 1986)
8. Lack of motivation and investment in learning (Swanson, 1991; Lehr & Harris, 1988; California, 1986)
9. Lack of social adjustment and social skills (Lehr & Harris, 1988; California, 1986)
10. Court-related problems (California, 1986)
11. Inattentiveness and short attention-span (Lehr & Harris, 1988)
12. Poor organizational skills (Lehr & Harris, 1988)

13. Dependency and learned helplessness caused by a lack of successful learning experiences (Swanson, 1991; Lehr & Harris, 1988)
14. Low average IQ scores (Wells, 1990)
15. Displays notable verbal deficiencies (Wisconsin, 1981; California, 1986)
16. Poor emotional health (Brodinsky & Keough, 1989)
17. Lack of self-discipline (Brodinsky & Keough, 1989)
18. Premature sexual activity (Brodinsky & Keough, 1989).

Community Related Characteristics

Lack of:

1. Responsive community support systems
2. Linkage between school and community services
3. Preventive mental health programs to address drug and alcohol problems
4. Family counseling
5. Community support for schools
6. "Neighborhood schools"
7. Adequate transportation
8. Ability to deal with the high incidence of criminal activity (Pasternak, 1986).

It is important to note that these characteristic indicators are interconnected and overlapping: they must be viewed in combination, not in isolation, when trying to determine if a student is at-risk (Wells, 1990).

One specific characteristic may not lead to low achievement; however, combinations of characteristics can be a better predictor of poor school success. In a study conducted by Frymeir, information was collected from 21,000 students in 276 schools across America. He found that if a child was at-risk in one area, the odds were overwhelming that the child was also at-risk in other areas. In fact, a child who was considered at-risk in any one particular area was almost twice as likely to be at-risk in every other area as a child who was not at-risk in the first area (Frymeir, 1989 & 1992).

80% of at-risk students are defeated & discouraged learners

Richard Sagor (1993) observes that 80% of the at-risk students in our classrooms receive the least amount of attention. These are the students that Sagor and Conrath (1986) call "the defeated and discouraged learners." Sagor believes the identification of at-risk students to be a complex and controversial process. By identifying the common characteristics of discouraged learners, we can form a picture of an at-risk student. Conrath (1986) states that these students:

1. Have low self-esteem and feel powerless and helpless.

2. Avoid school when possible. They find the school environment to be demanding, threatening and unresponsive to their needs. They find contact with peers and adults painful because of their lack of self-confidence. When they fall behind in their classwork they may avoid school altogether. Avoidance behaviors begin early in their school careers.

3. Feel mistrustful of adults and adult establishments.

4. Do not have a sense of the future, consequently, they are motivated more by short-term, measurable goals. They are not optimistic about the future.

5. By grades six and up, they are usually behind in their academic skills. They see themselves as dumb and tend to give up on their abilities to "catch up." They feel incompetent intellectually.

6. Have parents who suffer similar characteristics of low self-confidence and skills, distrust of institutions, discouragement and feelings of impotency. Many come from homes of poverty.

7. Conrath indicates these students often have adequate peer relationships; some are very lonely, and some choose friends for their ability to fill their needs for fun, support, and similar interests. Adults may disapprove of their friends.

8. Feel irritated with and intolerant of demands to sit and listen for lengthy time periods, as well as routines and boring classrooms. They are often disruptive and act out their impatience.

Lectures

9. Often come from the learning preference identified as "practical." They learn well experientially and can talk about it better than write about it. They do not retain information well when a lecture teaching style is used.

10. Tend not to see a relationship between effort and achievement. They are "externalizers" who find it difficult to accept responsibility for their actions whether they be personal failures or successes. They have poor "inner locus of control."

It is clear that over time, these reluctant learners become our at-risk population, who become, in turn, our school drop-outs.

11 risk factors with the highest predictive power

1. Poverty

Research indicates that students from economically disadvantaged families come to school with an array of characteristics that place them at a greater risk for failure. According to Natriello, McDill, and Pallas (1990), economic status and educational achievement are significantly linked. Bianchi (1984) found that children living in families with incomes below the poverty line were nearly twice as likely to be retained than children in non-poverty stricken families. **Applebee et al. (1988) found that by age nine, students in disadvantaged communities were already nearly a standard deviation behind in measures of reading proficiency on standardized tests than their more affluent peers. (A difference of this magnitude translates to the difference between the 16th percentile and the 50th percentile)**. The US Department of Education's "High School and Beyond" survey indicates that youths from families in the lowest socioeconomic quartile were more than three times more likely to drop out of school than those from families in the highest socioeconomic quartile (Roderick, 1993).

Most accurate predictors

Letgers and Slavin (1992) found socioeconomic characteristics to be the most accurate predictors for dropping out and for experiencing other school-related problems for preschool and kindergarten age children. They believe this is because of both the limited predictive validity of assessment tests for young children and their lack of practical school experience. As students move beyond the early grades, the most accurate predictors of negative outcomes become their actual performance in school: grades, attendance, and retention.

2. Poor Academic Performance

While poor academic performance is typically accompanied by other risk factors, it represents a very high risk factor in and of itself (Willis, 1987). **Poor grades are the most frequently reported reason given by dropouts for leaving school. Students who have been retained as a consequence of poor academic achievement are 40% to 50% more likely to drop out of school than students who were never retained (Bachman et al., 1971). In fact, one of the most easily measurable and reliable indexes of a student's risk for dropping out is whether youths were overage for their grade level by the time they enter high school** (Dryfoos, 1990).

Retention increases potential of dropping out

3. School Attendance

McDill, Natriello, and Pallas, (1990) examined the effects of higher academic standards on potential dropouts and found that the consistent failure and frustration of low academic achievement inevitably led to increased absenteeism, truancy, and school-related behavior problems. **Willis (1987) states that student attendance is undoubtedly the earliest and most visible indicator of potential problems in school and often begins at a very young age**. Since learning time and time-on-task are inexorably linked to school performance, it makes sense that the number of days a student is absent from school would be a significant predictor of low performance.

Important

4. Poor Self-Concept

A commonly reported result of underachievement and poor academic performance is a poor self-concept and poor self-esteem (Sartain, 1989). It is interesting to note that research also shows that teachers greatly affect children's self-perceptions. Silvernail (1985) states: "Students who feel they are liked and respected by their teachers have higher self-concepts, while those who believe they are disliked by their teachers are more dissatisfied with themselves" (18).

Educators must show they like and respect their students

5. Motivation, Locus of Control, and Risk-Taking

Student motivation is closely linked to self-esteem. Highly motivated students take credit for their successes and attribute their failures to things they control, such as effort. Poorly motivated students often attribute their successes to luck or factors out of their control, while they attribute their failures to low capability (Weiner, 1970). Since ability attributions have the greatest impact on self-esteem, individuals will feel best when success is attributed to ability, and, conversely, worse when failure is attributed to lack of ability (Wigfield and Asher, 1984). Highly motivated students exhibit an internal locus of control, while poorly motivated students exhibit an external locus of control. Payne and Payne (1989) report that a review of the locus of control research indicates that attribution is a key factor in school achievement.

Develop internal locus of control in students

Because at-risk students do not attribute successes to their ability, this leads to a drop in their willingness to take risks or to attempt challenging tasks, which, in turn, leads to low motivation. In other words, at-risk students' doubts about their ability to succeed makes refusing to actively participate in the learning process an attractive option. Thus, we can see that poor student academic achievement leads to problems with attribution, self-esteem, motivation, and risk-taking.

6. Antisocial Behavior

In an analysis of data from the U. S. Department of Education's "High School and Beyond" study, Ekstrom, Goertz, Pollack, and Rock (1986) found that behavior problems were, along with poor academic performance, a major factor when determining a student's probability of dropping out. Not surprisingly, then, antisocial behavior is closely associated with poor academic achievement (Sartain, 1989). In fact, according to one team of researchers, a quarter of slow readers displayed antisocial behavior, while a third of all conduct-disordered children demonstrated reading disabilities (Rutter, M. et al., 1970).

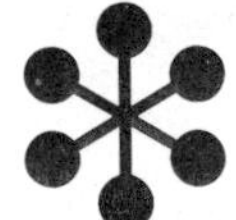

Poor reading and antisocial behavior are linked.

7. School Disengagement and Incongruence

Given the diversity of characteristics displayed by at-risk students, it is important to note that there are also important similarities between them that indicate both physical and mental disengagement from school. Negative attitudes towards school — often demonstrated early on — lack of participation in academic and social activities offered by the school, and truancy are all strong indicators of such disengagement (Willis, 1987). Tinto (1987) referring to the concept of incongruence as it relates to the process of school withdrawal, states that incongruence:

> refers to the general mismatch or lack of fit between the needs, interests and preferences of the individual and those of the institution . . . it springs from individual perceptions of not fitting into and/or being at odds with the social and intellectual fabric of institutional life (p. 53-54).

If students don't learn the way we teach,

we must teach the way they learn!

Tinto (1987) points out three situations in which incongruence may occur.

1. <u>A mismatch between the returns of continued schooling and a student's goals and expectations</u>. This is especially true if students do not find the content of classroom learning relevant to their lives (Fine, 1987; Whelage et al., 1989). Because of this, students may feel that their needs and goals may be better realized by joining the work force.

2. When the student feels marginalized and isolated either socially or academically. In a study done by Tidwell (1988), when asked what was the worst features of their high school, dropouts most often cited boring and uncaring teachers and crowded classrooms.

3. When there are role conflicts between school and the student's external community. This may be especially true for students who come from disadvantaged backgrounds. These youths are the ones who are more frequently making early transitions to adult roles, possibly due to an outside job, early pregnancy, or home crisis.

8. Educational Environment of the Home

In another analysis of the "High School and Beyond" survey data, Natriello (1987) found that problem behavior and grades appear to be determined in part by the home educational support system. This system includes the mother's educational aspirations for the student, the number of study aids available in the home, parental involvement in curriculum choice, and the number of opportunities for non-school learning. In fact, a study done by Rumberger (1983) states that the educational environment in the home is the most important determinant of whether or not a student will graduate from high school. After analyzing the research on dropouts, Roderick (1993) states that: **"Across studies, parental education, measures of the presence of reading material in the home, a parent's educational expectations for his or her child, and the degree to which parents monitor their child's education have comparatively the largest and most consistent impacts on the probability of dropping out across all race and sex groups"** (p. 33).

4 circumstances which impact students dropping out

9. Single-Parent Families

Research shows that students from single parent families face a substantially higher risk of dropping out of school. After controlling for income, parents' occupation and education, and other background characteristics, students from single parent families in the "High School and Beyond" survey were still 28% more likely to drop out than students from dual parent households (Barro and Kolstad, 1987).

10. Mobile and Transient Students

According to Coddington (1972), school transfers have been considered one of the most stressful and frequently occurring major life events that children undergo. Some studies show that in the United States, an estimated six million students between the ages of five and thirteen transfer to new schools each year (Cornille, Bayer, & Smyth, 1983; Schaller, 1975). Another investigation determined that only 20% of the sixth-grade population had been in the same school since first grade (Bensen, Haycraft, Steyaert, & Weigel, 1979). There is a predominant assumption that for some children changing schools may precipitate impairment of academic achievement (Lacey & Blane, 1979) and cause emotional and social problems (Holland et al., 1974; Turner & McClatchey, 1978).

School transfers are most stressful to children

Lacey and Blane (1979) also state that, as a result of school transitions, students' educational experience may become repetitive and boring and, also that moves may cause them to miss large portions of important academic work. Long (1975) writes that, despite previous academic success, transfer students may be required to catch up in some subjects. Thus, adjusting to a new school system is thought to be difficult for any new student, regardless of their past academic achievement or social development (Brockman & Reeves, 1967; Holland et al., 1974; Panagos, Holmes, Thurman, Yard, & Spaner, 1981).

In a review of recent research on the adjustment of transfer students, Jason et al. (1992a) found that there was not always agreement on how changing schools affected children. Jason found the research suggests that major life events such as school transitions may not directly cause psychopathology among children, and that these events are mediated by other sources of chronic stress; therefore, students exposed to multiple stressors probably run a greater risk for maladjustment.

Mobility and low SES can lead to significant learning problems

Additionally, children from low SES households who are thought to be exposed to multiple chronic stressors are more at-risk for maladjustment from school moves. According to Dohrenwend (1973), persons in lower social status groups are disproportionately exposed to stressful life events, which explains the links between low social status and high individual psychological distress. When students do not possess adequate personal and external resources to cope with multiple transitions, they are at a higher risk for encountering school difficulties (Jason, et al, 1992a).

Unfortunately, there is presently inadequate support in most districts for transfer students, especially for at-risk students (Jason, et al, 1992a). Several researchers cite this lack of comprehensive preventive interventions aimed at special-needs transfer students as a problem (Jason et al., 1989; Jason et al., 1992b; Felner, Ginter, & Primavera, 1982).

Within-District Scheduled Transitions

School transitions can be categorized into two types: scheduled, when whole groups of students enter school or move together to middle school or high school; and unscheduled, when single students change schools. Students transferring alone are unlikely to receive the benefit of planned orientations and adjustment periods which typify scheduled transfers. Jason, et al (1992a) supposes that, because of this, it is safe to assume that the academic and social adjustments of unscheduled moves are more difficult than scheduled ones. One study showed that students who underwent an unscheduled school transition during the summer were less effected than students who transferred during the school year (Brockman & Reeves, 1967).

Do you have a written transition plan as you move students in your district?

However, Roderick (1993) cites research that shows even scheduled school transitions are difficult periods for youths. He states that grades normally decline following a scheduled school move, particularly following the transition to high school. In fact, when looking at trends in the average grades of dropouts, Roderick found that it was largely following these scheduled school transitions that the academic standing of eventual dropouts began to

diverge from those of graduates. According to several researchers, school transitions consistently lead to a significant decline in average grades, regardless of the grade at which the student changed schools (Blyth and Simmons, 1987; Blyth et al., 1983; Crockett et al., 1989; Felner et al., 1981; Schulenberg et al., 1984).

Transitions to both middle and high school are distinguished from other kinds of school moves because they involve changes in the size and complexity of the physical environment, role, and the academic demands and organization of classrooms (Felner et al., 1981; Blyth and Simmons, 1987; Eccles, Lord, and Midgley, 1991) These types of transitions are also typified by less personal and more disciplined student/teacher relationships, greater use of whole class instruction (Eccles et al., 1991) and a higher likelihood of being tracked by ability than in elementary schools (Becker, 1987; Eccles et al., 1991). Using Tinto's theory of school withdrawal, Roderick (1993) suggests that the extent to which students encounter academic and social difficulties adjusting after the school transitions to middle and to high school may impose significant barriers to their integration into the school community. Declining grades during these crucial periods provide an overall index of a student's ability to successfully adapt to the new academic and social environment.

Caution: first year in middle school

> **Roderick states: *"I found that a student's performance during the first year of middle school had an important impact on the chances that he or she would drop out of school. Students who had difficulty during the first year of middle school were more likely to drop out even after including information on their school performance through the transition to high school"* (p. 101).**

11. Latch-Key Children

According to Woods (1972), inadequate after-school supervision has also been found to be associated with poor academic achievement and self-esteem. It has also been shown to have effects independent of those due to other forms of parent involvement (Muller, 1991b). An analysis of data from the National

Educational Longitudinal Study of 1988 containing a total sample size of 20,491 students in 802 public and 233 private schools found the following:

1. Disregarding all extraneous factors, students left unsupervised watch about 8 minutes more of television per hour than those who are supervised.

2. Students left unsupervised for less than an hour perform better on tests than students from other groups, especially those left unsupervised for more than three hours.

3. Students left unsupervised for longer periods of time also receive lower grades. This holds true even after controlling for other background characteristics such as race/ethnicity, family composition, and mother's employment status (Muller, 1991a).

Latch kids experience stress from being home alone for extended periods.

Contrary to expectations, this same study provided evidence which suggested that unsupervised students were not doing poorly in school because they were not doing their homework. Although students left unsupervised were watching more television, being home alone did not seem to affect the amount of homework they did. Muller postulates that students feel significant amounts of stress from being home alone for an extended period of time each day after school. This stress may then directly affect their academic achievement, as is evidenced by their lower grades and test scores.

Four Theories on "At-Risk" Students

Sagor (1993) believes that the first step of any successful at-risk program must begin with the articulation of a theory of its causes in a specific environment. There are four dominant theories found in the literature on at-risk students, each of which is briefly explained below.

Clinical Pathology Theory

The child or his/her environment is responsible

This theory, often called the epidemiological, medical, disease, or child-deficit model, presumes that the causes of children's failure in school reside primarily, if not exclusively, within the child's physical being. This perspective limits the characteristics and conditions that are considered. It presupposes that the risk factors are specific, innate inadequacies, limitations, incompetencies, and deficiencies within the child such as, hyperactivity or A.D.D., a learning disability and/or inadequacies due to deprived and unhealthy homes.

Developmental Deficit Theory

The educators must correct the problem

This theory holds that at-risk students have missed out on experiences or skills that they should have had in order to experience success. The task for the educator in this model is to determine what the missing skill or attribute is (i.e. self-confidence, social skills, academic skills etc.), and then to remediate the missing piece. Possible interventions would include the development of appropriate remedial/acceleration programs such as Chapter I, alternative schools, or young five programs. The assumption is that, once students acquire the needed skills, they will successfully return to and remain in the normal learning environment. The drawbacks of this theory are that students often never "catch up" to their peers, and that adequate data is not collected to determine the effectiveness of the interventions.

The institution is the problem

Institutional Pathology Theory

This theory sees at-risk students developing as the consequence of differential and inappropriate treatment by institutional forces. Rather than being on the students, the focus is instead on changing the institutions that are placing them at-risk, such as the school or the family. In this model, one might focus on changing the economic system which produces the poverty which helps to create at-risk students. Or, it may mean that schools begin to reevaluate certain school practices which have been shown by research to put students at a greater risk of failure, such as retention and tracking. Efforts at school restructuring would fit into this model.

There must be a balance & fit between the child and institution

Ecological Theory

This theory, which is interactional in nature, is similar to the institutional model but covers a broader scope. While it does not deny the existence of the characteristics that predispose most students to academic failure, it does assume that student failure must ultimately be understood as the consequence of students' interaction with their environment. Richardson, Casanova, Placier, & Guilfoyle (1989) describe this model as follows:

> It is an interactive view in which the perception of at-riskness is constructed within a particular social or cultural context. The child brings to the classroom a certain number of characteristics that have been shaped by background and personal factors, and past experiences in school. This child interacts with a classroom context that includes other children, teacher(s) and materials. In addition, what happens in the classroom is shaped, in part, by school level factors that are often influenced by district level factors. The focus in this approach is not on the child alone, but on the interaction between the child and these nested contexts (7).

As Donmoyer (1993) explains when describing this theory, it helps us to understand why a particular student may be considered at-risk by one teacher and not another, or by a teacher at one particular point in time, but not at another if a more "at-risk" student enters upon the scene. Johnson (1994) explains it in terms of a balanced ecosystem: **when the child's characteristics are compatible with the environment then the system is harmonious; conversely, when the child's characteristics are not compatible with the environment, the ecosystem is not balanced, and failure and dysfunction will occur. This theory never assumes that a child's character istics are absolute. Nor are they seen as deficiencies, inadequacies, or the cause of the at-risk behavior. Instead, these characteristics are viewed in terms of "the goodness of fit" between the child and the environment.**

What is the fit between the child and the environment in your school?

Schools often deal with at-risk students in ways that overlap in terms of theoretical models. Sagor (1993) recommends that once a district chooses the model it most believes in, and begins to brainstorm intervention strategies, it must first ask the following questions:

1. Is the proposed strategy consistent with our theory of at-risk behavior?
2. Is there empirical evidence to support our belief that it will work in this setting?

Sagor gives examples of schools which believe that there are flawed educational practices occurring; however, these schools still send at-risk students to alternative schools rather than dealing with the flawed mainstream school. Sagor states: **"Rigorous attention to the connection between our interventions and our beliefs can do a lot to prevent later frustration with disappointing results" (p. 260).**

Despite the difficulties with using identification models, it is widely held that early identification is a worthwhile goal. (Pallas, 1991; Frymeir, 1992; Wells, 1990). Since dropping out of school is the end result of a process taking place over the student's entire school career, it would benefit educators to take a closer look at the factors influencing that decision, which would have been building for the thirteen or so years the child had been

Early identification & intervention are important.

in the educational system In fact, since poor academic performance at an early age as well as grade retention at the elementary level have been shown to predict multiple problem behaviors in older children, it would seem that early identification and intervention would be worthy goals for districts interested in helping to keep at-risk students in school (Dyroos, 1987; Frymeir and Gansnider, 1989; O'Connor, 1988).

Traditional School Interventions

School districts have historically tried various approaches to intervene with failing students. This section documents these approaches and their effectiveness.

Retention

The majority of research has consistently shown that retention is ineffective and has few positive effects on a student's learning

One method for dealing with failing students has been to retain them at their present grade level. The majority of research has consistently shown that this practice is ineffective and has few positive effects on a student's learning (see Shepard & Smith, 1989 for a collected review). Tobias (1989) reported that if a student fails one grade level, the probability that he or she will drop out is increased by 50%. A study done by Grissom and Shepard (1989) attempted to analyze whether the retention decision itself increased the risk of dropping out, or if it was just another symptom of poor achievement. <u>They found that when student background, sex, and achievement were controlled, grade retention was still a significant factor in a student's decision to drop out. Because of this, they concluded that retention added to the risk of a student dropping out, stating:</u>

> Grade retention is a discrete policy intervention that appears to contribute to the drop out problem. Whether it is a part of a negative set of experiences that convince the student he can't make it or merely a temporal dislocation that makes the student too old for his classmates and a year further from grad-

> uation, the negative consequences of the extra year are clear. As noted by Rice et al. (1987), the repeat year would have to produce achievement gains of thirty months to compensate for the negative effects of being made a year too old (p. 61).

Schulz (1986) concurs and states that drop out rates for overage students are about 13 percentage points higher than for normal age students with identical reading achievement scores.

> Overage students must have reading scores over 2 grade levels higher than normal-age students in order to have the same chance of graduating. The rate of progress of low-achieving students is less than one grade level per year by definition. A year of remedial study cannot possible increase such students' achievement by over 2 grade levels (p. 9).

Being overage increases the risk of dropping out!

In fact, Roderick (1993) found that students who were overage for grade, regardless of whether they had been retained or not, ran a higher risk of dropping out throughout their school careers. Although she points out that her findings could by no means be considered conclusive, she emphasizes the importance of further research to investigate this question. If her findings on the negative results of being overage for grade can be further substantiated, then it would seem clear that early retentions do more harm than good. Also, if there is an effect of being overage for grade, then even retaining youths in order to help them overcome their academic problems would not mitigate the impact of that retention.

*** *Retention does not work***

A meta-analysis of 44 studies done by Holmes and Matthews (1984) which compared academic achievement and attitude, personal adjustment, behavior, and attendance found that, when compared to retained students, promoted students had:

1. significantly higher academic achievement
2. better personal adjustment
3. higher self-concept
4. more positive attitudes toward school
5. less absences than retained students.

In a separate meta-analysis, which included the above 44 studies plus an additional 22 studies, Holmes (1989) found that retained groups scored .19 of a standard deviation unit lower than the promoted comparison groups on academic achievement. This translates to a mean ES of -.31. This was true even when academic achievement was further subdivided into language arts, reading, mathematics, and social studies measures. The promoted comparison groups consistently outscored the retained groups in each sub-area.

According to both Byrnes and Yamamoto (1986) and Grissom & Shepard (1989), there seems to be clear indications that retention not only fails to solve academic problems, but is also associated with negative self-concepts in children, negative attitudes towards school, and a higher drop out rate. Swanson (1991) states:

> Educators are losers, also, when they retain students. We lose when we persist in a practice that is clearly damaging to students. We lose because it destroys our students' motivation to learn. We lose because it prevents us from seeking effective solutions to learning problems. We lose because our credibility is diminished when we engage in practices that are contrary to professional standards supported by research. As Frymeir (1989) put it, retaining students is unprofessional and unethical. (p. 60)

Educators are also losers when they retain students!

Kindergarten Experiences

There are several issues related to Kindergarten programs that affect the at-risk population. Each is reviewed below.

Full-Day Vs. Half-Day Programs

One major issue is whether full-day or half-day programs are better for children. A review of effective kindergarten programs and practices for at-risk students (Karweit, 1989 & 1992) explores the small number of quality research studies addressing this issue. Her review found only modest and sometimes inconsistent short-term benefits for full-day programs. These findings were most consistent in studies focusing on disadvantaged students. However, there was little evidence to substantiate the long-term effects of full-day kindergarten attendance. Instead, the use of time was found to be the most important issue; Meyer (1985), for example, found that some half-day kindergartens provided more high-quality time than full-day programs.

Kindergarten Entrance Age

One strategy routinely debated is the raising and lowering of the entrance age for kindergarten to help better prepare children for school.

Karweit (1992) found that studies on the effect of the age at which a child enters kindergarten did not support this strategy. While Shepard and Smith (1986) did find that the youngest children in the classroom scored lower on 1st grade reading tests, these differences disappeared by 3rd grade. In addition, Shepard and Smith discovered that the kindergarten population today is, on average, older than it was 30 years ago due to changes in the regulations which govern starting age.

Karweit (1992) proposes that moving the starting age simply defines another group of children as the "young" students, and that the major effect of the change in age over the last 30 years has been to accelerate the kindergarten curriculum.

Two year programs are a form of student retention

Two-Year Kindergarten Programs

Because children differ markedly in their readiness levels for school and in their rates of development, many districts have implemented two-year kindergarten programs. Considered as an extra year of preparation for first grade, two-year programs are, in actuality, a form of student retention. Three types of two-year programs exist: (1) developmental kindergartens, where children are screened prior to the first year of kindergarten and then placed in a pre-kindergarten room; (2) transitional first grade classes, where students having difficulty in regular kindergarten can spend an additional year before entering a regular first grade classroom; (3) and kindergarten retention, where a child is recycled through kindergarten after failing the first time through.

Despite the fact that the research unequivocally supports the conclusion that retention is an ineffective policy, proponents of kindergarten retention feel that retention at the kindergarten level is different. There are several reasons for this belief:

1. Students are retained before academic failure occurs, so kindergarten retention is seen as a preventative measure.
2. Students are often retained for immaturity rather than for poor academic skills.
3. Retention in kindergarten is not believed to carry the stigma associated with later retention (Shepard, 1989a).

Because of these differences, proponents of kindergarten retention deny that research conclusions showing the detrimental effects of retention at later grade levels are applicable to kindergarten. Therefore, it is necessary to look at separate studies aimed directly at the effects of repeating kindergarten.

Debate over Kindergarten retention

In a review of all available research on kindergarten retention in all of the three forms listed above, Shepard (1989a) asked if extra-year programs are effective, if they prevent subsequent failure, and if they improve achievement over what it would have been had the student not been retained. Most importantly, Shepard asked if kindergarten retention differs fundamentally from retention in later grades? In her review, Shepard included an earlier review by Gredler (a 1984 research review on transition rooms at the kindergarten level), as well as an expanded review of more recent studies. Evaluation and research reports from school districts identified by the Gesell Institute (1988) as having successful developmental programs were also included by Shepard. (The Gesell Institute is a proponent of early screening and placement of "developmentally young" students in a developmental kindergarten or transitional first grade room to gain an additional year to grow). Shepard's findings corroborated those of Gredler, as well as those of Mantzicopoulos and Morrison (1992) from a later study. Shepard (1989a) found that:

Kindergarten retention is ineffective

> **Although a year older than their new grade peers, transition children perform no better academically than transition-eligible children who went directly on to first grade. The finding of no difference or no benefit is true whether children were placed on the basis of immaturity. Children who spend an extra year before first grade are just as likely to end up at the bottom of their first or third grade class as unready children who refused the special placement.**
>
> **Academically able but immature children who repeat kindergarten may well be at the top of their first grade class but are not ahead of where they would have been without the added year, as shown by equivalent controls . . . Self-concept or attitude measures, only rarely included in research studies, showed no difference or negative effects from the extra-year placements. In this respect retention, whether it is called by a special name (transition), occurs for special reason (immaturity), or takes place in kindergarten rather than later, is still retention — and still ineffective (pp. 75-76).**

In addition to the above findings, which relate to student achievement in elementary school, it is important to remember the association between retention and dropping out of school (Tobias, 1989), which suggests that there are more harmful long-term effects to be considered. In fact, according to Lloyd (1978), **studies of students who have been retained before 3rd grade find that, controlling for their achievement, such students are far more likely than similar non-retained students to drop out of school.**

Chapter I Programs

Note: Chapter I has been renamed Title I. Since it is still referred to in the literature as Chapter I, it will continue to be called Chapter I in this review in order to avoid confusion.

The national Chapter I program is the largest federal education program providing extra help to students at-risk of failure, serving over 5 million at-risk students nationwide. Started in 1965, this program continues to be the primary source of funding for a wide range of academic and social programs.

Chapter I employs various delivery strategies, some of which are listed here.

1. **Pull-out programs:** students are pulled from their regular classes for 30 to 40 minute periods for remedial instruction in the subjects they find the most difficult. Classes usually contain less than eight students and are taught by a certified Chapter I teacher.

2. **In-class programs:** the Chapter I teacher or, more typically, an instructional aide, works with eligible students within the classroom.

3. **Add-on programs:** resources are provided outside of the regular classroom, such as summer school or after school programs, to help at-risk students. Some districts use Chapter I funds to provide pre-kindergarten programs or to provide full day kindergartens.

4. **Replacement programs:** Chapter I students are placed in self-contained classes where they receive most or all of their instruction.

5. **School-wide programs:** projects are created through which the entire student population in the building can benefit from Chapter I funds.

Pull out programs did little to close the gap & gains were not sustained over 2 years

The most widespread delivery strategy of Chapter I services is the pull-out model (Letgers and Slavin, 1992). Natriello and co-authors (1990) summarized several studies done in the mid-Eighties on pull-out programs and concluded that children in these programs displayed only modest positive effects on reading and math skills. They found that gains did little to close the gap between low-achieving students and their more advantaged peers, and that the progress that students did make was rarely sustained more than 2 years after participation in the program. An ongoing 1992 national assessment report which summarized research through 1988 noted that Chapter I appeared to improve basic skills but did not teach higher-order skills (Rotberg and Harvey, 1993), and that the improvements in basic skills were not sustained over time. Also noted in this report was that Chapter I programs were not integrated with regular school programs.

Rotberg and Harvey noted that, because of the diversity in service, the mixing of strong results with those that were modest or weak, and the use of tests which bore little relationship to Chapter I program in any particular schools, the actual evaluation results of the report provide little useful or meaningful information.

Rotberg and Harvey also observed that the expectation of notable academic progress through Chapter I services as they are typically used appears unrealistic: while a student gains an estimated 12 extra minutes daily in both reading and mathematics, this time is subtracted from the rest of the curriculum, primarily in reading and mathematics; therefore, it is not at all surprising that Chapter I programs achieve only modest short-term benefits.

Disadvantages of Pull-out programs

Pull-out programs are known to have several disadvantages:

1. There is a lack of coordination between what is taught in the regular classroom and what is taught in the pull-out program (Stein, Leinhardt, and Bickel, 1989; Natriello et al., 1990). This fragmentation of student learning can be particularly difficult for students who are low achievers by making the content seem unintegrated and meaningless to them.

2. Pull-out programs can lead to a reduction in classroom teachers' sense of responsibility for the academic welfare of educationally disadvantaged students (Natriello et al., 1990; Stein, Leinhardt, and Bickel, 1989; Swanson, 1991).

3. Chapter I students are often stigmatized and labeled as inferior in the eyes of their peers and teachers (Natriello et al., 1990; Swanson, 1991).

4. Continual interruption of teachers' instructional days causes managerial headaches when trying to plan class lessons (Stein, Leinhardt, Bickel, 1989).

Additionally, research suggests that the pace of instruction for low-ability students is slower, and that teachers focus more on low-level objectives and routine procedures than they do with high-ability students (Shavelson and Stern, 1981; Weinstein, 1987).

Special Education

Special education services have been offered to students identified with handicaps since the passage of the Education of all Handicapped Children's Act of 1975 (PL: 94-142). Services range from special schools to special classes within regular schools to various part-time placement programs. Instruction is typically provided to special education students in very small groups by teachers certified in special education.

According to Letgers and Slavin (1992), from 1976-77 to 1989-90 the number of students receiving special education services has increased 30.4%. Letgers and Slavin also found that, while the percentage of students categorized as physically disabled and mentally retarded has stayed at about the same level over this period, the number of students categorized as learning disabled (LD) increased by more than 250%. Letgers and Slavin (1992) state:

Startling

> Almost 90% of this increase represents the entry into the special education system of low achievers who would not have been served in special education in the Seventies. In other words, special edu-

Should this practice be continued?

cation has assumed a substantial burden in trying to meet the needs of students at-risk of school failure. Yet research comparing students with mild academic handicaps in special education to similar students left in regular classrooms finds few benefits for this very expensive service (see Leinhardt & Pallay, 1982; Madden & Slavin, 1983, p. 15).

While some researchers suggest that as many as half of the more than 1.8 million learning disabled children are inappropriately labeled (Algozzine & Ysseldyke, 1983; Shepard, 1987), others believe that it is difficult to distinguish between learning disabled and low achieving students (Shepard & Smith, 1983; Shinn, Tindal, Spira, & Marston, 1987). Cummins (1984) opines that learning disabilities are not coherently defined and that there are no valid measures of these conditions. This seems likely since estimates of their incidence vary inexplicably from 2% to 20%. Two qualitative studies which examined the referral and diagnosis process in LD cases found it to be lacking in objectivity and often socially constructed rather than scientifically determined (Mehan, Hertwick and Heihls, 1986; Smith, 1983).

$pecial education co$t$ are increa$ing at a phenomenal rate

Aksamit (1990) warns that, with the costs of identifying, placing, and serving handicapped students increasing at a phenomenal rate, it will be difficult for special education funding to keep up with the demand. She also cautions that this continued reliance on special education as a catch-all for at-risk children could actually result in inadequate services for these students in whatever type of school environment they are placed. In addition, special education funds for more seriously handicapped students could also eventually be jeopardized due to a lack of funds.

Mildly handicapped students who are in special classrooms for part of their school day are also likely to experience some of the same problems as students of Chapter I pull-out programs — a lack of coordination between regular classroom instruction and what is taught in special classrooms, a reduction in their class room teacher's sense of responsibility for student's academic welfare, stigmatization and labeling; and lost time as students move from class to class.

Curriculum Casualties

Are you creating "curriculum casualties" in your school

Some researchers believe that most of the students who are currently being labeled as learning disabled are, first and foremost, victims of defects in the school system (Hargis, 1989; Gickling and Thompson, 1985; Tucker, 1985). Hargis (1989) calls these normal but low achieving students "curriculum casualties." The curriculum is often lock-step in nature, laid out in a segmented hierarchy of objectives sequenced from kindergarten through the twelfth grade; this type of hierarchy often employs commercially prepared materials, which only help to reinforce this lock-step curriculum. Shannon (1983) notes that despite this, these materials are given an enormous amount of credibility. Under-achieving children, although they may enter school at the same chronological age as the other students, may not be as ready or have the learning abilities to benefit from such a rigid curriculum.

In this system, <u>if the student doesn't keep pace it is seen as the child's problem, not the schools.</u> This seems true especially because the majority of students do well in the programs. Additionally, the three or four high achieving students in every classroom will be forced to proceed at a level well below their capabilities. High achievers are sometimes allowed to break from this lock-step arrangement by accelerating their progress, whether through the process of skipping grades, compressing course work, "testing out" of courses, early graduation, and/or early admission to college or college courses. Even if the reverse takes place, and low achieving students are allowed to decelerate their pace and move through the curriculum at their own learning rate, rigid demands for grade level performance may cause them to experience failure anyway.

Often, when tasks become too difficult for low achieving students, they usually do not have the inclination or the time to finish them. This is important because the amount of time spent in what is known as "academically engaged time" is directly related to achievement. Emmett Betts first studied this idea in 1946, finding that **when students do not understand around 4% of the words in a reading selection, their comprehen-**

Interesting information on off-task behavior!

sion drops and they begin to show signs of off-task behavior. In turn, this increases students' frustration level and represents the point at which failure could be said to begin. **In drill and seat work activities, the frustration level begins when students are unable to do more than 30% of an assignment** (Hargis, 1989). Continued failure results in a variety of learned error patterns and ineffective approaches to learning. For these students practice will not make perfect: in fact, they will probably not improve at all academically, and may actually become worse. Stanovich (1986) and Hargis et al., (1988) call this the "Matthew Effect," where "the rich get richer and the poor get poorer." Eventually, a student trapped in this pattern will require remedial instruction, which is both time consuming and labor intensive. **Ineffective learning patterns have to be detected, unlearned, and replaced with appropriate strategies**.

Grading

Origin of the bell curve

In the early part of this century, Daniel Starch introduced the normal system — or what we call the bell curve and the ABCDF system — to school grading (Farrell, 1990). According to Wallace and Graves (1995), the curve was discovered by Carl Friedrich Gauss of Germany and originally appeared in the nineteenth-century. Gauss pointed out that there were natural occurrences which tended toward an arithmetical average. For example, the weight of adult geese or the girth of fifty-year old men could be plotted on a graph with a vertical axis representing numbers and a horizontal axis representing weight; this graph would then produce a bell-shaped curve with the peak of the curve representing the average. This Gaussian curve occurs frequently in the distribution of both natural and chance events. Wallace and Graves (1995) clearly state the problem with applying this same curve to education:

> In reality, however, many natural characteristics do not produce bell curves but irregular, skewed curves. This is usually true, for example, of human accomplishment: for the age at which men marry, the patents held by inventors, the number of publi-

> cations of research scientists, the amount of music written by composers, yearly earnings — and student achievement (Mensch and Mensch, 1991). This is because human accomplishments are more a function of will and effort than of inherent, naturally occurring qualities such as intelligence. Educators, however, assume achievement reflects intelligence more than will or effort. Most instructional practices stem from this assumption. Students are grouped by age for mass instruction on the assumption that their academic abilities will describe a bell curve. Since most fall in the average range under the dome of the curve, most can profit from group instruction geared to that average. Or so the theory goes (pp. 17-18).

Is this assumption predominate in your school?

Thus second grade teachers, for example, teach to the average reader — those who can read a simple sentence at the beginning of the school year — even though they may have students who are still mastering letters, sounds, and beginning words, as well as those who are independent readers. Similarly, publishers produce textbooks geared to the average student in that particular grade level. **Because of this, the artificially produced bell curve in the classroom is a self-fulfilling prophecy**.

Wallace and Graves (1995) feel that this approach is inappropriate for the approximately 30% of students who do not fall under the dome of the curve, into the average category. They list three flaws in this structure:

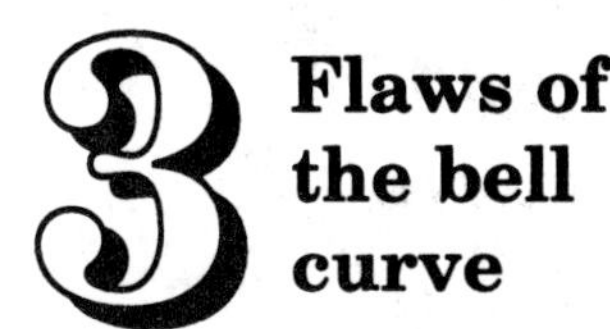

1 Instruction and expectations are geared to average levels, which tends to be mediocre. It is not likely that a system geared towards mediocrity will produce anything other than that.

The system is obsessed with the average, creating an evaluation system that judges students more on how they compare to the average than on what they actually know. This is a system that pits students against one another and promotes the myth that every class will include some students who are smart enough to make it and some who are not. "In a system that judges students on their relative performance, no one can look good without someone looking bad. It is literally impossible for all students to succeed" (p. 26).

The institutionalization of the bell curve by the public education system has made it a <u>prescriptive rather than a descriptive tool.</u> The curve is seen as a law of nature and, along with tracking and other practices, forces students into a bell-curve pattern of achievement whether it fits them or not. Teachers who grade on a curve rank their test scores in the following way: the top 7% receive an "A," the next 15% receive a "B," the middle 56% receive a "C," the next 15% receive a "D," and the bottom 7% are given an "F." The resulting curve balances the high grades with an opposing number of low grades regardless of how much or how little the class as a whole learned. **This brings the purpose of our entire grading system into question: is it to gauge learning, or to sort students?**

Do administrators do this in your district?

Another difficulty with grading is that administrators typically expect to see the semblance of a bell curve when teachers grade. Traditionally, a teacher who gives all "A" grades is likely to be questioned, while those who give too many "D" and "F" grades are often seen as too demanding. Wallace and Graves (1995) believe that administrators have allowed the bell curve to shift or skew toward the high end in the last thirty years; while student achievement has remained static over the last decade, grade averages continue to climb.

Grades also inevitably vary from school to school, which only seems to add to the confusion. A panel of educators reviewing federal remedial education programs stated:

> Today, in the absence of standards, grades on report cards overstate the performance of students in high-poverty schools, misleading students and parents and concealing the urgency for reform. On average, seventh-graders in high-poverty schools who received "A"s in math scored around the bot-

tom third (35th percentile) on the math standardized test, far below the national average. By comparison, "A" students in low-poverty schools scored at the 87th percentile. Indeed, an "A" student in a high-poverty school would be about a "C" student in a low-poverty school (US Department of Education, 1993, pp. 41-42).

Ability Grouping and Tracking

One common and far-reaching consequence of the bell curve phenomenon in both classroom organization and grading is tracking. Students who fall behind in curriculum content are usually dealt with through some form of ability or performance grouping, which is the practice of placing students from more heterogeneous classes or groups into more homogeneous classes or groups for either part or all of their instruction.

Placing students in separate classes, or tracking, has been frequently condemned in the literature. According to Slavin and Braddock (1993), research evidence is conclusive on this issue. When studying homogeneous or tracked classrooms, researchers discovered:

4 reasons why tracking doesn't work

1. Students in low groups are exposed to substantially less material, taught more low-level basic skills, moved at a slower pace, and exposed to less interesting and less challenging instructional techniques (Barr & Dreeben, 1983; Hallinan, 1987; Slavin & Braddock, 1993).

2. Tracked students' progress is retarded compared to that of similar students in heterogeneous classrooms: opportunities for progression are limited, instruction is generally inferior, and placements are self-perpetuating, often permanently locking students into an inferior track(Swanson, 1991).

3. Such placement assaults students' self-image and motivation (Swanson, 1991). A recent longitudinal study by Jomills Braddock compared low achievers in a tracked setting to low achievers in a heterogeneous setting. He found that low-track students had lower self-esteem and performed significantly poorer on achievement tests. Additionally, they were much less likely to end up in college preparatory programs than similar low achievers in untracked schools (Braddock, 1993). Students placed in the lowest "track" were also more likely than low achievers in mixed ability classes to feel powerless, become delinquent, and drop out.

4. Teacher's problems are compounded in homogeneous classrooms by the need to attend to so many needy students. Also, there is an absence of positive role models for low achieving students (Swanson, 1991). Possibly because of this, the standards for both behavior and attention have been found to be lower in homogeneous classrooms than in heterogeneous ones (Eder, 1981).

The research on performance-level grouping within the classroom is more ambiguous. Slavin & Braddock (1993) caution against eliminating all forms of grouping. They found that flexible within-class grouping can provide additional assistance to students who need help. Furthermore, they note that there is evidence to support the use of regrouping according to reading performance across grade lines. Research has also shown that gifted students, typically the top 3% to 5%, benefit from advanced placement and acceleration programs.

Flexible

Cross-grade grouping for reading is effective

Regarding within-class grouping, Swanson (1991) warns that unless teachers view performance levels as temporary and unless assessment practices are used correctly, tracking may occur even in heterogeneous classrooms. However, grouping students based on performance levels is not a problem in itself: the problem arises when students placed into these lower groups never catch up (Quality Education for Minorities Project, 1990). These students become locked into a given performance level and their educational opportunities are thereby limited. Additionally, some of the same factors that are counterproductive for grouping outside of the classroom may also hold true for performance level grouping within the classroom, depending on how this grouping is handled.

Continual assessment and reforming groups is important

There are those who oppose the de-tracking of our schools (Kulik, 1993; Gallagher, 1993). Their arguments center on the effects of programs for the gifted: while there is general agreement that acceleration programs are effective, it is more difficult to find reliable research which supports the more common pull-out enrichment programs for gifted children. **The major difficulty lies in the comparisons which are made in the studies**. Comparing students chosen for gifted enrichment programs with students who are bright but not accepted into the program is biased towards the accepted students; factors such as motivation, achievement, and classroom behavior can be reasons for a student's rejection. Conversely, using standardized achievement tests to compare the two groups of students is biased towards regular classroom students since they tend to do well on these tests, anyway. At any rate, as Slavin & Braddock (1993) maintain, such programs apply to only 3% to 5% of students:

> No serious reviewer suggests that there are educationally important positive effects of comprehensive ability grouping plans for a broader range of high achievers (for example, the top 33% of students). Even if there were evidence in favor of enrichment programs for the gifted, there would still be no evidence whatsoever to deny that such enrichment programs might be effective for all students, not just gifted ones (p. 14).

Reduce Class Size

Simply changing the number of students in a classroom cannot, by itself, be expected to change achievement levels.

Reducing class size is a highly charged emotional issue which has been debated since the 1920's. It is Slavin's (1990a) opinion that although parents and teachers both want the smallest possible class sizes, 50 years of research contradicts the belief that there is a connection between class size reductions and major gains in student achievement. The excellence in education movement has fostered a renewed interest in the issue of class size. Some states, including Indiana and Tennessee, are studying and implementing a reduction in class size in an effort to achieve educational excellence. In order to understand the debate on this topic, it is important to look at the history of the research as well as the latest findings from states such as Indiana and Tennessee.

In 1978, a meta-analysis done by Glass & Smith (Glass, Cahen, Smith, and Filby, 1982), brought the issue of class size to the fore. These researchers claimed that there was reason to believe that small classes could raise student achievement. However, Slavin (1990a) notes that of the 77 studies comparing larger and smaller classes, Glass et al (1982) found no effects in 63 of the inadequately controlled studies. Claims made by Glass and Smith are based on 14 studies which included tutoring situations from 1 to 3 students as well as one in which the subject taught was tennis. In a reanalysis of the Glass & Smith findings, Slavin eliminated the tennis study, several studies with 30 minute treatment durations, as well as three studies using college samples. He still found that dropping class size from an average size of 31 to an average size of 16 gained only a trivial effect size of .04.

In 1986, ERS conducted an updated review of the class size literature (Robinson & Wittebols, 1986). These researchers found that in grades 4-8 slight gains were found, while in grades 9 - 12 achievement gains were basically nonexistent. Gains in grades K-3 were more consistent: however, of these studies, only 50% found significant achievement differences in small classes, with all but one of the rest showing no differences.

Slavin's (1990a) analysis of class size research concluded that smaller classes do have more positive effects than large ones, but the effects are small to moderate in size. Slavin also found in a review of four longitudinal studies that there was not a cumulative effect of small class size. The effects seemed to diminish over periods of from three to six years. In another review of the research on this subject, Goettler-Sopko (1990) found considerable agreement that smaller class size seems to result in higher achievement among students who are economically disadvantaged and also in those with lower academic ability. However, if class size reductions for such students are accomplished through pullout programs, there are several studies which show that the negative aspects of the pullout situation may mitigate the positive effects (Cooley and Leinhardt, 1978; Kimbrough and Hill, 1981; Doss and Holley, 1982).

Effects diminish over time

Two state studies were implemented simultaneously, Tennessee's STAR Project (1985-89) and Indiana's Project Prime Time (1984-87). Results from the two studies seem contradictory. Indiana's Prime Time concluded that three years in a reduced class size produced little effect on primary student's academic achievement (Gilman & Tillitsky, 1989). Project STAR, on the other hand, concluded that there was a clear advantage to small classes over larger classes in raising academic achievement in the primary grades (Word, Achilles, Bain, Folger, Johnston, and Lintz, 1990). The larger effects found in Project STAR are concentrated mainly in kindergarten and first grade (Folger, 1990). After first grade, the effects of a small class level off and then decline, with about a 50% drop off in fourth grade (the first year students were back in regular class sizes of 21-28). In a study of why the two state projects produced such varying results, Underwood & Lumsden (1994) criticized the STAR project, stating that politics were greatly involved in the implementation. They also raise the possibility that The Tennessee Association of Education influenced the STAR project results. Additionally, Underwood & Lumsden found after investigating the STAR project that there was a strong probability of a Hawthorne effect (experimental group teachers trying harder to make students from small classes outperform those from the larger classes). Conversely, they also found a high probability of a John Henry effect where teachers of large class sizes would not try as hard to gain better stu-

dent performance. Underwood & Lumsden also found that neither state project was implemented with a "scientific attitude".

Many researchers seem to agree on one point: simply changing the number of students in a classroom cannot, by itself, be expected to change achievement levels (Mitchell and Beach, 1990; Slavin, 1990a; Goettler-Sopko, 1990).

Changed teaching and learning behaviors must accompany the reduced class size to obtain achievement gains. Teachers must be adaptable and have the skills and motivation to capitalize on the intervention. Even in the Tennessee project STAR, instructional methods of teachers with smaller class sizes remained virtually unchanged, suggesting that teacher training to take advantage of the benefits of smaller class sizes would also need to be considered.

Cost could increase by 33% with no real change!

It seems unlikely that school districts will be able to sell the idea of smaller class sizes given the current research findings and the cost of such an undertaking. Folger (1990) found that for Project STAR there was about a one-third increase in per pupil costs to reduce class size by one-third. These findings concur with an estimate by the U.S. Office of Education (Gilman, 1993) that found that reducing every public school class size would increase educational costs by 33%. This would include 73.3 billion dollars per year in teachers' salaries, 47 billion dollars per year in indirect costs such as instructional materials and building expenses, and would call for the hiring of an additional 1,365,821 teachers. Tomlinson (1989) warns that this action could cause some "unintended consequences" such as exacerbating the teacher shortage, causing a decline in teacher quality and producing inflationary bidding for teachers.

In a summary of class size research, ERS (1978), along with Karweit (1983), concluded that **the critical factor is the method and quality of instruction rather than the raw number of students in class.** Slavin (1990a) suggests that there are other more feasible alternatives that will produce larger effects than halving class size.

Mitchell and Beach (1990) suggest three distinct strategies for possible reduction of class size, including:

Redeploying staff: Creative management of existing staff resources through the shifting of staff workloads (i.e. principals, reading specialists and librarians teaching regular academic curricula to small groups of students for portions of the school day).

Redistributing students: Grouping students in more efficient ways (i.e. eliminating tracking of students within the classroom, and using peer tutors and team teaching techniques).

Incorporating small class instructional strategies: Such as ". . .better utilization of space, more individual interactions, and enhanced teacher "with-it-ness". . . lower noise levels, fewer discipline problems, more one-on-one instructional time, and more response by teachers to diverse student interests and abilities (p. 4)".

It is clear that the debate over reduced class size will continue. It is impossible to think about reducing class size without looking at how it would be funded. As Folger (1989) states:

Cost is a critical factor

> In a period of great concern about improving student achievement while controlling cost increases, class size reduction will need to be targeted to specific outcomes, and connected with an overall strategy for change. Unless that can be done, the high cost of across-the board class size reduction will be prohibitive (p.131).

Discipline Policies

As was noted in a previous section, behavior problems are frequently exhibited by at-risk students, and the discipline policies chosen by school districts can increase the likelihood that at-risk students with behavior problems will continue in a downward spiral. According to Roderick (1993), discipline problems and conflicts with school personnel emerged as important factors for males in their decision to drop out of school. She found that males were much more likely than females to report that expulsion or suspension contributed to their decision to leave school.

Sending students home may create more of a problem!

There has been little other research on the extent to which suspension, as a policy, may contribute to overall disengagement from school and school failure (Roderick, 1993). However, as Fine (1993) states, policies that send students home, causing them to miss classes and leaving them unsupervised when their behavior problem clearly shows that they need more supervision, may actually exacerbate these students' difficulties.

Wehlage and Rutter (1986) argue that, even if discipline problems are associated with low SES and other background factors, it is still crucial to view school failure as growing out of conflict with and estrangement from school norms and rules. Clearly, a change in school policies and practices that address this conflict and estrangement is necessary. In a review of the "High School and Beyond" survey, these same authors found that, taken as a whole, the responses of a broad range of students who were asked about the effectiveness and fairness of discipline policies were consistently negative. This data suggests that schools have a serious problem with how all students view the discipline system.

How do educators in your school demonstrate they are interested in the students?

The same "High School and Beyond" survey also brought two other interesting facts to the surface: first, students perceived teachers as having little interest in students themselves; second, only 8% to 10% of eventual dropouts actually anticipated doing so before reaching the 10th grade. This information suggests dropping out is not a conscious decision on the part of students that can be identified in the early years of high schools, but may in fact be caused by a combination of feelings of being rejected by their teachers and persecuted by the discipline system. Wehlage and Rutter state:

> Taken as a whole these data suggest that school factors related to discipline are significant in developing a tendency to drop out. . .The process of becoming a drop out is complex because the act of rejecting an institution as fundamental to the society as school must also be accompanied by the belief that the institution has rejected the person. The process

> is probably cumulative for most youth. It begins with negative messages from the school concerning academic and discipline problems (p. 385).

Wehlage and Rutter conclude by reemphasizing the necessity of reforming the discipline system to avoid creating a sizable group of deviants who see no alternative to resisting the school's authority that enables them to retain their dignity other than dropping out. They point to case studies of effective alternative programs for marginal students, which indicate that such students respond positively to an environment that combines a caring relationship, personalized teaching with a high degree of program structure, and high yet attainable expectations (Wehlage, 1983).

Elements Of Successful At-Risk Programs

Obviously the problems for our at-risk youths are complex and diverse. Clearly, the solutions for these problems will also be complex, diverse, and vary from district to district depending on their diverse needs. No single solution will meet the needs of all students in this population, thus each district and school will need to commit itself to the self analysis and the development of individualized and multifaceted solutions. Research on effective programs gives us some general guidelines to follow. Manning (1993), summarizes seven essentials that are present in the most successful programs. They must:

1. "Be comprehensive in nature by addressing more than one at-risk condition. Doing this greatly enhances the success of at-risk programs since few, if any, at-risk conditions result from a single factor.

2. Recognize the significance of self-concept as it relates to achievement and prioritize improving self-concept.

3. Maintain high expectations for at-risk students regardless of their at-risk factors.

4. Attend to students' social skills by teaching those needed to interact successfully.

5. Provide opportunities for teachers and learners to agree on educational objectives and methods for reaching them, indicating to the learner that educators genuinely want to assist them in their academic and social progress.

6. Include parents and families when setting program goals and the means to accomplish them.

7. Pay attention to the link between motivation and success and place substantial responsibility on the learner." (p. 135-138)

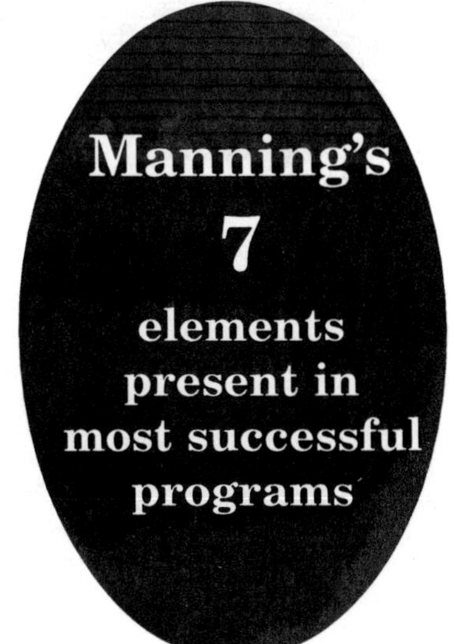

12

common elements of successful at-risk programs

In an additional summary of findings from successful program evaluations done by many researchers, Baas (ERIC Digest, 1991, p. 1) lists the following elements:

1. **Begin prevention early-in kindergarten or first grade.** Dollars spent on early intervention can yield up to a six-fold savings on the potential future costs of dealing with children who drop out.

2. **Aggressive leadership** by school boards, superintendents, principals, and teachers is needed to make things happen.

3. Parents are crucial and should be incorporated in any manner possible.

4. Specific solutions must be **school-based** rather than delivered from above, and should be woven into a **comprehensive K-12 program** (Hamby, 1989).

5. **Remedial programs are out**. Rather, stress high ethical and intellectual standards matched to realistic, attainable goals. **Offer an "alternative strategy for learning, not an alternative to learning"** (Conrath, 1989).

Staff development needed

6. **Teachers and principals need the training, encouragement, and "empowerment" to become active decision-makers.** All participants should understand precisely how they fit within a clear, predictable structure in which strategies can be adapted to meet each student's specific needs (Levin, 1987).

7. **Teaching should focus on continuous progress in language skills and emphasize problem-solving and teamwork.** Teachers need to be tough, compassionate, and professional. They also need to possess a strong sense of how to relate to the particular cultures represented among their students (McCormick, 1989).

8. Classes and, when possible, schools need to be smaller to facilitate interaction and one-on-one contact with students. A positive school climate is a must.

9. Districts and state departments of education should serve as resources and encourage decision-making to be made where it counts, at the local level. Principals should be freed from bureaucratic tasks to work more closely with teachers and students (Levin, 1987).

Principals must be instructional leaders

10. **Students should never be allowed to disappear into anonymity.** The school environment should be a place in which students are esteemed for their unique abilities and strengths (Hamby, 1989).

11. Educators should integrate their own services and goals with those of the basic social and health services in the community (Wehlage, Lipman & Smith, 1989).

12. School leaders need to mobilize the entire community. Businesses, senior citizens, clubs, and service groups may all provide extra funding, resources, and volunteers to work with students (Slavin, Karweit, & Madden, 1989, p. 1).

Gary Wehlage, National Center on Effective Secondary Schools at the University of Wisconsin, believes that schools sometimes contribute to student failure because of inadequate and incomplete responses to students. Wehlage and a team of investigators studied 14 schools and educational programs designed for students considered to be at-risk for dropping out of school. They reviewed a variety of data that included student achievement scores in reading, mathematics, and writing, along with psychological measures such as student self-esteem, locus of control, and social bonding. The result of their work is a theory of drop out prevention that can be applied to other at-risk programs. The components of this theory include the following:

Tailor to student needs

1. A successful drop out prevention effort must tailor educational responses to the specific situations of students.

2. Schools that are effective at educating at-risk youth recognize some basic psychological needs. One of the most

Social bonding is important for at-risk students

important of these needs, especially for at-risk students, is the need for social bonding, which involves four elements:

a. **Attachment;** student are "attached" when they feel that they have social and emotional ties to teachers and peers.

b. **Commitment:** students who conform to school rules and regulations demonstrate commitment. It allows students to tolerate rules that may be personally unsatisfying because they believe in the rewards that lay ahead.

c. **Involvement**: students who are involved in school activities see their involvement as valuable, meaningful, and legitimate. Involvement checks the boredom and passivity which leads students to drop out on a psychological level and, eventually, on a physical level.

d. **Belief:** students must believe in the school, the efficacy of education, and their ability to receive an education and to eventually graduate.

Wehlage Rutter, Smith, Lesko & Fernandez (1989) list practices which they believe are necessary elements in the formation of school membership and social bonding:

Elements for school membership and social bonding

1. Active efforts to create positive and respectful relationships between adults and students.
2. Active communications of concerns about and direct help for students with their personal problems.
3. Active help in meeting institutional standards of success and competence.
4. Active help in identifying a student's place in society based on a link between self, school, and one's future.

Current School District Responses To At-Risk Students

The school reform movement has resulted in the development of a variety of possible remedies for the problem of at-riskness. Some interventions have shown promise and are backed by research; others are more controversial and have received less support from researchers. In this section, some of the most prominent interventions are described and evaluated.

In At-Risk Students: Reaching and Teaching Them, Richard Sagor (1993) states, "There are certain psychological factors that, while applicable to people of all ages and stations, must be clearly understood and internalized before we can respond to the problems faced by our at-risk students." He then goes on to relate interventions he believes to be successful for at-risk youths, organized by their ability to meet these psychological needs. Sagor describes these psychological needs which are taken from research on primary human emotional needs by researchers ranging from Maslow to Glasser, as four central feelings which are critical to an individual's emotional well-being. They are described here as they relate to students' lives and feelings:

4 critical elements for emotional well being

1. **Competence:** How capable students feel in their role as learners.

2. **Belonging**: How accepted students feel by their peers, teachers, and staff.

3. **Usefulness:** The extent to which students feel they are making a difference in the lives of others.

4. **Potency:** The feelings students have about their ability to effectively make changes in their lives.

Youths who feel inadequate as students, unwanted by friends, unneeded by society, and powerless over their lives would have little motivation to behave positively or to persevere in school.

The following list of current school interventions is grouped in relation to their ability to create a school climate favorable to developing the four psychological factors identified on the previous page.

Mastery Learning

Feelings of competence in school comes from repeated success at meaningful and seemingly difficult challenges. Tracking, remedial programs, or other approaches that "dummy down" the curriculum do not typically cause students to feel competent and, in fact, often have the opposite effect. One mechanism for enabling all students to succeed with a single rigorous curriculum is Mastery Learning.

Benjamin Bloom (1976), the pre-eminent mastery learning researcher, argues that, "what any person in the world can learn, almost all persons can learn if provided with appropriate prior and current conditions of learning (p. 7)." Mastery Learning theory differs from traditional classroom theory in the expectations that are held for all students. With Mastery Learning, the poor performance which is a given with the "bell shaped curve" is reduced almost to the point of elimination. Additionally, high performances, once achieved by only a small portion of the class, now become the norm. **When Mastery Learning techniques are used, 50 percent more students will perform at the level of our A and B students** (Sagor, 1993).

Bloom states that 1 to 2 percent of students learn faster than the average student, while 1 to 3 percent will learn more slowly. These differences are due to background characteristics such as heredity, home environment, and in the case of the slower student, organic or functional disturbances. Accordingly, Bloom points out that 95 percent of our students are capable of learning what they need to learn if teachers carefully and systematically

apply appropriate instructional means (Bloom, 1976). These means are identified by Sagor (1993) as four critical variables of Bloom's Mastery Learning.

4 critical variables of Mastery Learing

Variable 1: Motivation

We must do all that we can to make students see the mastery of our curricula as a desirable end. If students see no value or purpose in acquiring mastery over the material, they will not be open to new learning tasks. The degree of confidence with which learners approach tasks is also important. It affects the amount of effort which will be put forth, as well as how obstacles and problems are dealt with.

Variable 2: Prerequisite Skills

This variable requires that teachers teach first things first. If students are missing critical skills which are prerequisite to those being taught, then the students are set up for failure when they are asked to proceed. Teachers must assess what students know then fill in the missing learning gaps. Remedial classes are not the answer if they slow down the learning process. Accelerating the learning for at risk students will make it possible for them to catch up with their peers and move ahead to learning new skills.

These first two variables are essential to providing an effective learning environment. In fact, according to Bloom (1976), **". . . up to two-thirds of the variance on achievement measures can be accounted for by the combined effects of these entry characteristics" (p.171).**

Variable 3: Quality Instruction

For students to acquire new skills they will still need quality instruction, even if they have the motivation and all the prerequisite skills. Quality instruction must be appropriate for learners in that it matches their learning style, their culture, and their cognitive level. Students need opportunities for active participation, reinforcement of learning, feedback, and corrective measures.

Variable 4: Adequate Time

This variable addresses the concept that given adequate time anyone can learn a skill or acquire knowledge. Our differences are based not so much on intelligence or ability as on the different time requirements we each have to learn a new skill. This frees up teachers to see their students differently. A student who is slow to learn math concepts may be fast when learning to read.

2 forms of Mastery Learning

According to Ellis & Fouts (1993), there are two forms of Mastery Learning which share common elements. The first form is called individualized instruction, which is based on the concept of continuous progress. This allows students to work at their own pace. Formative evaluation procedures are established as checkpoints along the way, with corrective activities provided for those learners who initially fall short of the established criteria.

The second form of Mastery Learning is known as group-based learning. This form is the one most closely associated with Bloom's work. It employs many of the Instructional Theory Into Practice (ITIP) strategies promoted by Madeline Hunter, which involve reducing learning into manageable objectives, teaching to those objectives, establishing formative evaluation activities, reteaching when necessary, and implementing summary-based assessment.

Research on the efficacy of Mastery Learning in the school environment is considerable and largely positive. In separate syntheses of Mastery Learning research, both Block and Burns (1976) and Guskey and Pigott (1988) reported that **students using Mastery Learning were not only learning more, but felt better about school and themselves as a result.** Bloom and associates (1984) consistently found results which indicated that **students in group-based Mastery Learning situations raised their achievement one standard deviation above the mean.**

Outcome-Based Education

Although Mastery Learning and Outcome-Based Education (OBE) are sometimes thought to be synonymous, they are actually not the same thing. The two hold similar tenets, however, they are implemented at different levels. Mastery learning, as defined by Benjamin Bloom, is a micro-level process implemented in the classroom as part of the teaching/learning process. OBE, a macro-level process, involves overall planning and restructuring of school or district policy. **Mastery Learning is a vital component of OBE.**

The OBE model begins with a process of determining the outcomes that are considered crucial for exiting students to acquire. The curriculum and instructional program is then organized around these skills.

This process differs dramatically from traditional school practice, where objectives are written for a curriculum which is already in place. As Ellis & Fouts (1993) state: "The existing curriculum must carry a burden of proof against the desired outcomes"(p. 97).

The 4 Premises of OBE

To understand OBE more fully, one must understand the underlying philosophical premises it holds. Ellis and Fouts (1993) state the following:

1. **All students can learn and succeed.**
   Student differences in learning come from the distinct ways students learn and the varying rates they learn.

2. **Success influences self-concept** which in turn influences learning and behavior. **It is a cause-and-effect relationship**, with **academic achievement the cause and improved self-concept the effect**.

3. **Schools control the conditions of success;** therefore, schools can change to improve the learning process. In this regard, one problem of the traditional instructional process is that objectives and measured outcomes are often unrelated. Educators often do not test what they teach.

4. **"Schools can maximize learning** for all students by:
   a. establishing a school climate which continually affirms the worth and diversity of all students,

   b. specifying expected learning outcomes,

   c. believing that all students can perform at high levels of learning,

   d. ensuring that all students have opportunities for personal success,

   e. varying the time for learning according to the needs of each student and the complexity of the task,

   f. having both staff and students take responsibility for successful learning outcomes,

   g. determining instructional assignments directly through continuous (formative) assessment of student leaning,

   h. certifying educational progress whenever demonstrated mastery is assessed and validated" (Ellis & Fouts, 1993 p. 93).

Spady's Principles of OBE

Bill Spady, known for his work with Outcome-Based Education, defines OBE in terms of four principles (Brandt, 1992a).

1. **Clarity of Focus:** All curriculum design, instructional delivery and assessment design are geared to what schools want students to demonstrate successfully at the end of their educational journey.

2. **Expanded Opportunity:** Students are given more ways and chances to demonstrate at high levels what they have learned.

3. **High Expectations:** Students are expected to succeed, thereby eliminating the traditional bell curve standards.

4. **Design Down:** Educators start where they want students to end up and work down to the curriculum level from there.

Despite the appeal of the OBE concepts, there is not a great deal of research documenting its effectiveness. According to Evans and King (1994), much of the existing evidence in support of OBE is largely perceptual, anecdotal, and limited in scale. Difficulties in assessing the effectiveness of OBE lie in an inability to document a universal definition of OBE.

Also causing difficulties for OBE researchers are obstacles educators find in their attempts to assess students. Many of the outcomes chosen by districts require complex measurement techniques. Also, OBE philosophies require that outcomes be significant and related to life roles. These high-quality outcomes culminate in demonstrations of significant learning in context. An outcome is not then a score or a grade, but an end product of a clearly defined process that students carry out. **Comparing student achievement in this new method with traditional measurements of student achievement can be difficult.**

Difficulties in assessing OBE

In an attempt to evaluate the research on OBE, Evans and King (1994) looked at specific OBE implementation and its effects at the state level. Data collected in Utah, Missouri, and Minnesota suggest the following three themes: OBE is effective at the classroom and the building levels; OBE is readily adapted into traditional systems, as indicated by successful implementations of OBE in Utah and in Missouri; and OBE benefits underachieving students, while having questionable effects on overachieving students.

Jonhson City Model

One example of an Outcome-Based Education program currently in place at a district level is the Outcomes-Driven Developmental Model (ODDM), which was started in 1972 in Johnson City, New York. Johnson City's ODDM, which uses an instructional model similar to Mastery Learning, has been quite successful. Johnson City is a lower-middle-class community with the second highest poverty rate of the 10 urban districts in its county (Evans and King, 1994). Statistics prove just how effective Johnson City's program has been (Evans and King, 1994):

It worked in Johnson City!

1. When the program started in 1972, Johnson City ranked last of the 14 district in its county in academic achieve-

ment as measured by standardized tests, and only 45% to 50% of its students scored at or above grade level in reading and math in the 1st through 8th grade. By 1977, that percentage rose to 70%, and in 1984, it was between 80% and 90%.

2. In 1976, 44% of all students performed at six months or more above grade level in reading, and 53% in math. In 1984, the figures rose to 75% in reading and 79% in math.

3. On the New York State Regents' Exams, 70% of Johnson City students participated in 1989, compared with only 58% of students county wide and 40% of students statewide. Additionally, 77% of Johnson City students received a Regents' diploma, compared to 59% and 43% of students county and state wide, respectively. When the New York Board of Regents instituted more rigorous requirements for a Regents' diploma in 1988, 55% of Johnson City students received the diploma, compared with 47% and 33% of students county and state wide, respectively.

4. For the 1991-92 school year, 100% of Johnson City High School freshmen were enrolled in algebra.

Opposition to OBE

A discussion of OBE would not be complete without a presentation of opposing arguments. Listed below are some of the main objections to OBE.

Affective Goals: The opposition fears that affective outcomes — which they feel require their children to have "politically correct" beliefs — will undermine their children's' Christian values and will have a detrimental effect on their grades. Many are afraid that affective outcomes are ambiguous and open to interpretation. There is also concern about possible subjectivity when assessing whether or not an affective outcome has been met.

Concerns About Indoctrination: The opposition believes that schools using OBE are indoctrinating children with social, political, and economic values in many subject areas. They worry that OBE will make covert indoctrination overt, and that teachers will feel free to share political perspectives antithetical to those embraced by the opposition. Opponents argue that schools become coercive when they mandate affective domain outcomes for all students.

Given the scarcity of hard data, the above research only shows that there is a clear need for additional research. The above researchers suggest that there first needs to be a clear definition of OBE, a determination of what exit outcomes are desired for students, and a method to accurately document student achievement.

Authentic Assessment

Testing is another area which can undermine at-risk students' sense of competency. Students, especially at-risk students, often do not see a connection between what is tested and what is taught, or between what is tested and real world experiences. Educators have also recognized the limitations of assessment systems which rely on multiple-choice standardized achievement tests. According to Schwartz and Viator (1990), norm-referenced, standardized tests often discriminate against low-income, minority test takers.

Such assessment systems used to ensure accountability, often encourage teachers to "teach to the test," thereby narrowing the curriculum and diminishing the validity of information gathered. Although this practice may result in raised test scores, **Herman (1992) found that superficial changes in instruction specifically implemented to improve test performance are not likely to result in meaningful learning.** Herman feels that the result of this phenomenon is that scores no longer represent broader student achievement, but only the content and formats included on the test because teachers are providing daily skill instruction in formats that closely resemble the tests. He has also found these effects to be amplified in schools serving at-risk and disadvantaged students, since they are under intense pressure to raise students' test scores.

What's happening in your school?

Which of the 3 is most commonly used in your school?

Three Most Common Types of Assessment

Norm - Referenced Tests: This form of testing compares a student's achievement with a local, regional, or national norm group. Their scores, which are statistical estimates based on the bell-shaped curve, provide information on how well a student performs in comparison to other students in the norm group. This form of testing is ineffective in assessing student learning of local curricular content since it is not covered on the test. Also, since norm-referenced test are paper-pencil instruments, they are limited in their ability to assess process skills and higher order thinking (Reed, 1993).

Criterion - Referenced Tests (CRT's): These tests measure students' attainment of specific skills or learning out-comes. CRT scores measure students against a standard rather than against other students. Usually objective in nature since they are multiple choice, true-false, or matching, many teacher-made tests fall into this category, as do some state-level exams.

Performance - Based Assessments: This type of assessment requires students to demonstrate specific skills or competencies in an open-ended situation (Reed, 1993). Shepard (1989a, pp. 6-7) lists several indicators of good performance-based assessments.

1. Assessment tasks should be designed to more closely resemble real learning tasks.
2. Tests should require more complex and challenging mental processes for students.
3. They should acknowledge more than one approach or one right answer.
4. They should place more emphasis on uncoached explanations and real products.
5. Structured formats should be changed often enough that there can be no benefit to practicing a skill in one particular format.
6. The dimensions of the test domain must be expanded so that teaching to the test does not imply teaching only a subset of learning goals.

In order for a performance-based assessment to be authentic, it must have some connection to the "real world" or a simulation of that world. Authentic performance assessments are also integrative in nature, simultaneously measuring many different facets. They may be individual, but are often group-based (Bergen, 1994). **When they are group-based, both individual and group performances are evaluated. This form of assessment requires students to know more than just one right answer.** As Reed (1993) states, "They represent a synergism in learning: the total effect is greater and more fluid than the sum of the discrete parts that compose it." (p. 12)

This last testing form, authentic performance-based assessment, has been suggested by Sagor (1993) as an effective method to use with the at-risk population. Some of the reasons for this belief, according to Marzano (1994, p. 44), may be because performance assessments:

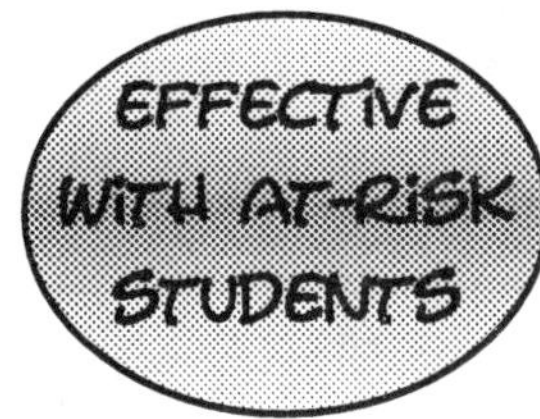

1. Provide clear guidelines for students about teacher expectations (Berk 1986)
2. Reflect real-life challenges (Hart, 1994),
3. make effective use of teacher judgment (Archbald and Newmann, 1988)
4. Allow for student differences in style and interests (Mitchell, 1992; and Wiggins, 1989)
5. Engage students more than other forms of assessment (Wiggins, 1991).

Marzano (1994) claims that, contrary to traditional multiple-choice, fill-in-the-blank, and/or true/false assessment tools, performance-based assessments provide information about students' abilities to analyze and apply information.

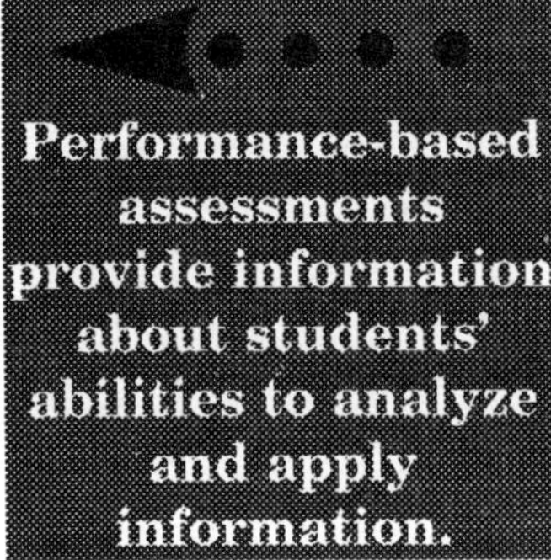

Marzano (1994, p. 44) clearly summarizes Resnick's (1987) argument for performance assessments:

> Many of the tests we use are unable to measure what should be the hallmark of a "thinking" curriculum: the cultivation of students' ability to apply skills and knowledge to real-world problems. Testing practices may, in fact, interfere with the kind of higher-order skills that are desired.

In recent years, there has been an intense interest in the educational field in performance-based assessment. Guskey (1994) cites two major reasons for this: first, advances in cognitive science (Resnick 1985 and 1987) have caused educators to acknowledge that learning is complex and requires diverse means to assess it fully and fairly; second, advocates of authentic assessment believe that improved assessment devices will naturally call forth higher quality instruction. This would be especially true if the assessment taps higher-order thinking skills, thereby producing instructional practices that emphasize and develop such skills.

Rubrics are essential for effective assessment

Marzano (1994) also addresses the question of reliability. Interrater reliability refers to the extent to which independent raters agree on the scores assigned to students when tested for various proficiencies. Marzano reports a high reliability on content specific performance tasks, and Shavelson et al. (1993) note that performance assessments in mathematics and science are highly reliable in their scoring. Researchers have found that performance tasks that have rubrics written specifically to the proficiencies assessed can be scored quite reliably. Conversely, tasks whose rubrics are very general cannot be scored reliably (Marzano, 1994).

Measuring validity, or the extent to which the performance assessments measure what they are supposed to measure is more complicated. Performance tasks are commonly considered to have strong "face validity," meaning that they appear to measure what they are supposed to. However, some researchers warn that this is not enough (Linn and Baker, 1991).

Because these assessment techniques are fairly new, much more data needs to be collected not only on the technical quality of the assessments, but also on their reliability as measures of student learning. **Despite this lack of data, researchers seem to agree that authentic testing shows definite promise** (Herman, 1992; Marzano, 1994; Ellis and Fouts, 1993).

Thinking Skills Programs

Thinking skills programs have become quite popular in education over the last ten years. However, the terminology defining these programs is quite loose. Various terms associated with thinking skills include: critical thinking skills, higher order thinking skills, problem solving skills, strategic reasoning skills, and productive thinking skills.

It seems obvious that thinking skills are very important. In fact, if it could be proven that they could be taught successfully, students would develop a sense of competency in their academic careers. Since at-risk students are often grouped separately with a focus on basic skills, it would be advantageous to them if a way could be found to effectively teach them higher-order thinking skills. Unfortunately, there are many difficulties in proving the claims of program advocates. A few of these difficulties, listed below, are pointed out by Ellis and Fouts (1993) in their book, Research on Educational Innovations.

1. There is little agreement about what thinking skills actually are. The abstract concepts about and loose definitions of particular skills make it extremely difficult to conduct research proving program efficacy.

2. Measuring thinking skills is difficult, if not impossible. The validity of current tests have not been agreed upon and define various constructs differentially. There is still much work that needs to be done in designing stable, acceptable instruments for assessing thinking.

3. It has not been proven that thinking skills can be taught successfully to students independent of content. Thus, it is not certain that transfer will take place to other subjects or applications. In fact, research done by Bransford et al. (1986) states that enhancement is limited to the specific domain that was the focus of instruction, and that there is little in the way of cross-domain transfer. How then do we construct content-free tests that will truly measure thinking skill acquisition?

Many believe thinking skills can be taught. . . but we don't have definitive data to support it!

4. Teachers themselves may not possess these various thinking skills, and, if they do not, they cannot teach them to students. This is an area that needs additional study and research: to what extent do teachers have these skills, and how prepared are they to teach them?

5. Little is really known about how people actually think. According to Baer (1988), it is not completely clear whether thinking is a conscious or an unconscious process. This makes it difficult to determine if we are actually able to teach people how to think.

Even with the aforementioned difficulties, thinking skills programs abound. The thinking skills movement seems to have branched into two forms: the adoption of specific curricula or programs such as Talents Unlimited, Higher Order Thinking Skills {HOTS}, Odyssey, Strategic Reasoning, Instrument Enrichment, Cognitive Research Trust {CoRT}, Project Impact; and the development and implementation of a matrix of thinking skills intertwined throughout the school curriculum. Many of these programs involve substantial teacher in-servicing.

Ellis and Fouts (1993) state that quality evaluation studies documenting the effectiveness of these programs are nearly impossible to find. While there are many anecdotal stories claiming success, there are few in-depth analysis. Sternberg and Bhana (1986) evaluated five programs and found most of the research to be weak in design and possibly biased; they found the research results to not only be inconclusive, but also ineffective at pointing out specific ways in which programs did or did not succeed.. Ellis and Fouts warn: **"This is a very lucrative in-service and materials area, and it preys on the vulnerability of professionals of good will who so much would like to improve the quality of students' thinking. We make no claim that these programs fail to produce thinking skills in students. We just do not have strong evidence that they do." (p. 142)** On the other hand, they also state: **"There is so much in the way of interesting, intriguing activities in the various thinking skills programs, especially if the activities were undertaken by students in, say, cooperative learning groups, that we would encourage you to review**

them yourself. Even if the result is not higher test scores, you still may find yourself saying the activities represent time well spent." (p. 143)

Multicultural Education

Sagor indicates a sense of belonging is a significant psychological need important to all students, especially at-risk students. To create a sense of belonging for students in the school community, we must create an environment where they feel welcome, valued and an important part of the social fabric of the school. The following approaches and interventions have been cited in the research literature as effective means to help students gain this sense of belonging.

When children come to school and do not see the culture of their home and/or neighborhood around them, they do not develop a sense of belonging. While many of today's schools are home to a rich and diverse student population, those that are not can look forward to a remarkable transformation in the youth of our country. According to Natriello et al. (1990), "while about 7 in 10 children in 1988 were whites, only about 1 in 2 will be in 2020" (p. 37). Based on statistics compiled in 1986, the number of children speaking a primary language other than English will double — from 4% to 8% of our school-age population — by the year 2020.

How prepared are you to deal with this cultural diversity ?

Based on prior experience, we will see a substantial increase in our at-risk populations because of a corresponding projected rise in the number of children living in poverty. In 2020, educational institutions will serve 4 million more children who live in poverty than they served in 1987 (Natriello et al, 1990).

Multicultural education is one strategy for creating schools where all students feel they belong. James Banks, a prominent writer in the field, describes multicultural education as a process whose major goals are to help students from diverse cultural, ethnic, gender, and social-class groups attain equal educational opportunities, and to help all students develop positive cross-cultural attitudes, perceptions and behaviors (Banks, 1989). Banks (1993) describes multicultural education as a complex and multidimensional concept which includes the following elements:

Teachers use content integration when they use examples, data, and information from a variety of cultures and groups to illustrate the key concepts, principles, generalizations, and theories in their subject area or discipline. Superficial celebrations of heroes and holidays, or one day cultural festivals, trivialize multicultural education, conveying the idea that it's acceptable to notice diversity in a single event.

Multicultural education should include the following

When teachers help students understand different perspectives and how these perspectives influence people's conclusions they are using the knowledge construction process. Banks 1994, suggests that the structure, assumptions and perspectives of the curriculum be changed so that the subject matter can be viewed from the perspectives and experiences of a range of groups. This method, Banks asserts can:

a. teach students about our differences as well as our similarities
b. bring content about currently marginalized groups to the center of the curriculum
c. help students understand that people construct knowledge based on their experiences, values, and perspectives,
d. help students construct knowledge themselves
e. help students grasp the complex group interactions that have produced our culture.

In this approach students would study the Civil Rights movement from both black and white perspectives, and the settling of the West from both Native American as well as European American viewpoints.

Reducing prejudice helps to develop a sense of belonging

Prejudice reduction occurs when efforts are made to help students develop positive attitudes about different racial groups. According to Phinney and Rotheram (1987), although children enter school with many negative attitudes and misconceptions about different racial and ethnic groups, education can help students develop positive views of other races, creeds, and religions.

However, this can occur only if instructional materials with positive images of diverse groups are used in consistent and sustained ways (Banks, 1991).

The modification of teaching techniques and strategies which facilitate academic achievement among students from diverse groups will develop a sense of belonging. **Teachers must believe that all students can learn. Apple (1990) and Winfield (1986) found that teachers expect more from white students than from black students, as well as more from middle-class students than from working and lower-class students. When teachers believe a student will underachieve, they usually will (King and Ladson-Billings 1990; Lipman, 1993).**

Potential is so completely unknown to us, we dare not underestimate any child!

Schools need to look at their grouping practices, social climate, assessment practices, extracurricular activity participation, staff expectations and responses to diversity. Sagor (1993) refers to these school aspects as "the hidden curriculum." Sagor also believes that if we have a fully integrated professional staff we empower minority youths to feel recognized and to be hopeful about their futures.

Learning Styles

Learning style theorists believe that all individuals have modality strengths which have been influenced by both heredity and environment. These modality strengths translate into a preference to learn in a particular way. This learning style preference may include a partiality to learning and communicating visually, orally, spatially, and tactiley. It may also mean that certain students may learn better in a quiet or an active environment, a formal or a relaxed setting, with others or alone, or even in some combination of these. Some learning style advocates believe that at-risk students have the most to gain from matching their learning styles to those of teachers because these students' styles seem to be the ones that differ the most from the predominant learning style in our schools (Sagor, 1993; O'Neil, 1990).

Learning styles may help the most with at-risk students

In an article from Educational Leadership (O'Neil, 1990), Harvey Silver, of Hanson, Silver, Strong, and Associates, says, "At-risk students learn best through direct actual experience, cooperation and collaboration, and high levels of interaction. As you go up the grade levels, school becomes more competitive, more independent, more abstract. We've designed a system that works directly against them." (pp. 5-6) Some cite increasingly diverse student populations, as well as high drop out and student disengagement rates, as reasons for the heightened interest in applying style theory in the classroom. It is believed that focusing on learning styles might be one way to enable teaching methods and curricula to reach more students (O'Neil, 1990).

The implications of learning style theories for the classroom vary somewhat. According to some advocates, it is imperative that we identify student learning styles and match them to teacher instruction (Dunn, Beaudry, and Klavas, 1989). However, others feel that this approach would further handicap our at risk students. Sagor (1993) suggests that we help at-risk students to become ambidextrous in regards to learning styles, thereby increasing their probability of success in a work world filled with a broad range of styles. Sagor finds the McCarthy 4MAT system helpful in striking a balance between a child's need to have their individual style accommodated and their need to stretch what he calls their "style comfort zone." McCarthy proposes that teachers systematically vary their style of instruction in order to meet these two student needs. It has also been suggested that teachers could construct each daily lesson geared towards a different style or teach each subject in a different style at different times. The idea is that, in doing so, no student will feel alienated for an extended period of time, while simultaneously receiving experience in all other learning styles.

Sagor finds 4Mat System to be helpful.

Unfortunately, as appealing as the concept of learning styles may be, there seems to be numerous obstacles to its implementation, as well as insufficient substantiation of research claims made by learning style theorists. Another major problem is discovering any particular student's learning style. While a variety of assessment instruments exist to do this — the best known of which include the Myers-Briggs Type Indicator, the Learning Styles Inventory, and the Embedded Figures Test — all of the available instruments which attempt to discover learning styles have been plagued with troubles of both validity and reliability (Ellis and Fouts, 1993). One difficulty with such tests is the ambiguity of the meaning of learning style: in a factor analysis of four instruments, Ferrel (1983) found that each of the instruments were actually measuring different characteristics.

There have also been questions about the claim that instruction based on learning styles increases learning. Ellis and Fouts (1993) cite the following problems with the existing research supporting the use of a learning styles approach:

Problems with the research supporting learning styles

1. The experimental designs employed in research on classroom-based learning styles are weak to nonexistent, with inadequate controls (O'Neil, 1990).

2. The researchers may be biased by possible "mercenary" interests (Kovale and Fourness, 1990).

3. The Hawthorne Effect, generated by the enthusiasm of doing something new, invalidate any findings.

4. The studies were conducted by graduate students preparing their Ph.D. theses under the direction of faculty members who had a vested interest in substantiating a particular learning styles conceptualization (Curry, 1990).

5. The validity and reliability of the assessment instruments are questionable (Curry, 1990).

6. The learning styles theorists are unable to distinguish learning styles constructs from intelligence research (Curry, 1990).

Teaching students the best way for them to learn is a worthy goal for educators to pursue. However, as Ellis and Fouts state:

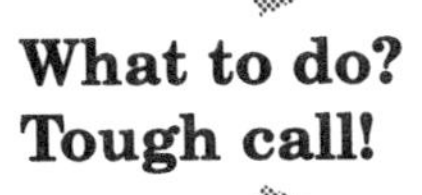

> Many of the strategies identified for teaching and learning by learning styles advocates make perfect sense. However, at this point, we feel that the burden is on the learning styles theorists to provide a clearer sense of the beneficial outcomes of a learning-styles based approach before we would suggest that you jump on this bandwagon. Certainly a decision to change methodologies or to do wholesale retraining of teachers based on the research in this area would be a mistake because neither the quantity nor the quality of empirical evidence is there (70).

New Findings About Intelligence and Brain Theories

Multiple Intelligence

Gardner's 7 Intelligences

Educators' belief that there is such a thing as a limited, measurable and innate capacity to learn has done much to deleteriously effect students' sense of belonging. This aptitude, called intelligence or IQ, has effectively limited opportunities for countless students who do not test high on IQ exams. In the last several decades various researchers have been reexamining the commonly held definitions of intelligence. Howard Gardner of Harvard has become well-known for his theory of multiple intelligences. According to Gardner (1983), there are at least seven separate intelligences: linguistic, musical, logical-mathematical, spatial, bodily-kinesthetic, and inter and intra-personal. Gardner has found that individuals can be gifted in one area while seemingly quite ordinary in another.

Robert Sternberg of Yale has developed a theory of intelligence based on work he has done regarding information processing. According to Sternberg (1990) there are six factors which define our ability to process information effectively, and consequently to think productively. They are spatial ability, perceptual speed, inductive reasoning, verbal comprehension ability, memory, and number ability. Sternberg's work emphasizes the thinking processes that may be common to everyone. He breaks cognitive behavior into thinking, adapting, and problem solving. Emerging from the work of both these men are new perceptions of what intelligence and thinking skills are.

Sternberg's 6 factors define ability to think productively

The evidence that intelligence can be learned and developed and that it is not innate and immutable supports the mastery learning research which was discussed in this text on page 52-53. Given adequate time, quality instruction, the necessary prerequisite skills and the motivation to learn, all students can achieve. Given the work being done in the area of intelligence, it is important for educators to have an open mind about the meaning of IQ scores and the idea that intelligence may not be defined in the near future in the same ways as it has been defined in the past.

Brain Research

In the last decade, dramatic developments in brain research have been challenging educational practices in our classrooms and schools. Robert Sylwester, a professor at University of Oregon, cautions educators that, "When these brain theories and their strong supporting evidence shortly reach general public awareness, educators will be asked to comment on them. Because their thrust raises fundamental issues about our professional assignment, we'd better understand them" (1994 p. 15)

Are you prepared for this?

The following principles are just a few mentioned by Caine and Caine which give a general theoretical foundation for brain-based learning and, "help us to reconceptualize teaching by taking us out of traditional frames of reference and guiding us in defining and selecting appropriate programs and methodologies" (1990 p. 66).

Principle One: The Search for Meaning is Innate
The brain constantly and naturally searches for the familiar while concurrently seeking out the novel (O'Keefe and Nadel, 1978). For educators, this implies a necessity to provide stability and familiarity along with novelty and challenge. The innov-

ative methods used to teach gifted students are good examples of this process, and Caine and Caine suggest they should by utilized for all students.

Principle Two: The Search for Meaning Occurs Through "Patterning"

Patterning critical to learning!

The brain has a natural capacity for integrating information into a pattern and, in fact, resists unrelated or seemingly meaningless material (Lakoff, 1987; Rosenfield, 1988). The implication for educators is critical. Since we cannot stop this pattern-making, we need to try to influence it in natural ways. "For teaching to be really effective, a learner must be able to create meaningful and personally relevant patterns" (Caine and Caine, 1990 p. 67). This research supports the use of thematic teaching, real-life tasks and assessments, and hands on experiences.

Emotions are crucial for storage and recall of information

Principle Three: Emotions are Critical to Memory

Not only are emotions and cognition inseparable (Ornstein and Sobel, 1987; Lakoff, 1987), but they are crucial for the storage and recall of information (Rosenfield, 1988). In our schools and classrooms, therefore, the emotional climate becomes of prime importance. Cooperative learning, where mutual respect and acceptance are stressed, is supported by this research.

Principle Four: Our Memory System Includes Both Spatial Memory and Rote Learning

Our **spatial memory** system allows for "instant" memory of experiences (Nadel and Wilmer, 1980). This system is always engaged, is motivated by novelty, does not need rehearsal and drives the search for meaning. Our **rote memory**, on the other hand, is designed to store unrelated pieces of information (O'Keefe and Nadel, 1978). This information must be worked on or rehearsed before it can be stored. "The more information and skills are separated from prior knowledge and actual experience, the more we depend on rote memory and repetition" (Caine and Caine, 1990 p. 68). For educators, this means moving away from focusing on memorization of facts (multiplication tables, spelling words etc.). These techniques do not facilitate the transfer of learning and make it difficult for students to create meaningful connections to what they are learning.

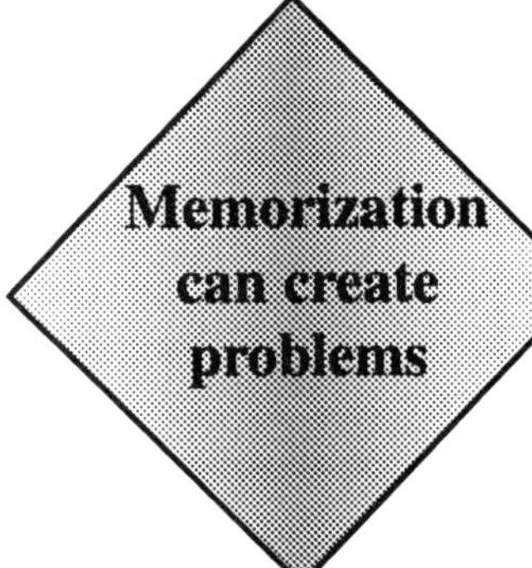

Principle Five: Learning is Enhanced by Challenge and Inhibited by Threat

"Downshifting" occurs in the brain when there is perceived threat (Hart, 1983). Perceptual fields are narrowed, according to Combs and Syngg (1959), and we become less flexible and more automatic. Consequently, teachers need to provide a highly challenging environment with a minimal amount of threat. Caine and Caine (1990, p. 69) suggest creating a "state of relaxed alertness" in students.

These are just a few of the findings from the brain research. Because this research is complex and comprehensive, several excellent books are recommended, including: Teaching and the Human Brain by Renate and Geoffrey Caine; A Celebration of Neurons by Robert Sylwester; and Emotional Intelligence by Daniel Goleman. It is clear that this research will provide educators with information which will have far reaching effects in every area of education.

Cooperative Learning

Sagor's third psychological need is the need to feel useful and to make a difference in the lives of others. Unfortunately, the traditional classroom setting is often individualistic and competitive in nature — we have moved a long way from the one room school house where older students taught younger students and the more skilled student tutored the less skilled.

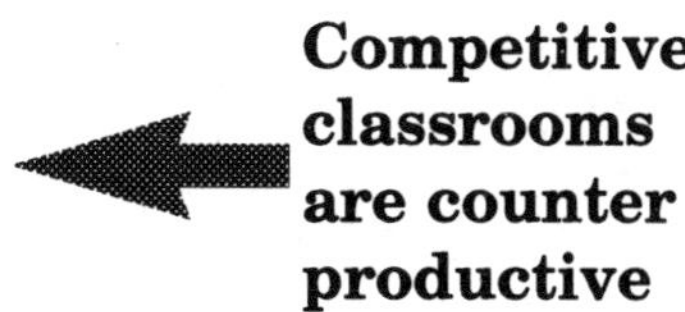

Sagor (1993) states that many educators and progressive social theorists have become concerned about the damage individualistic, competitive classrooms may cause. Sagor cites research (Johnson and Johnson, 1990; Peters and Waterman, 1982; and Senge, 1990) which claims the competitive classroom model, in which students compete against classmates, has proved to be counterproductive not only in the school setting, but in the workplace as well. Sagor states "The social groupings we live and work in supply us with status, reinforcement, and reaffirmation of our value. Therefore, our feelings of usefulness will be derived or denied as a consequence of the quantity of meaningful and purposeful interactions we have with others" (103).

One way to create a sense of usefulness in students is the use of Cooperative Learning in the classroom. In Cooperative Learning, the typical classroom teaching and learning activities are supplemented in such a way that much of the individual seat work is replaced. According to Goodlad (1984), students initiate classroom discussion an average of only seven minutes per day. Cooperative Learning provides many more opportunities for students to interact and to develop interdependence. Consequently, students feel a greater sense of usefulness they feel that they are a critical part of both the learning process for themselves and others. Although Cooperative Learning takes on many different forms in the classroom, all of its forms share the same basic premises: students working in groups or teams to achieve specific educational goals, and students learning to rely on one another by developing positive inter-dependence. Four major models of Cooperative Learning are briefly described below.

Cooperative learning gives students an opportunity to feel useful

4 Cooperative Learning Models

1. **Learning Together Model**: developed by David and Roger Johnson of the University of Minnesota, presents a framework in which cooperative, competitive, and individualistic learning can be used as an integrated whole.

2. **Student Team Learning:** developed by Robert Slavin of Johns Hopkins University, uses the motivation of team competitions where strong and weak players work together to reach a common goal.

3. **Group Investigation:** developed by Shlomo Sharon and Yael Sharan from the University of Tel Aviv, it involves six stages in the group investigation process, which occur over several weeks to a month. It also includes a general plan for organizing a classroom using a variety of cooperative strategies.

4. **Structural Approach:** developed by Spencer Kagan of the University of California-Riverside, it includes ways of organizing social interactions in the classroom with the sole purpose of getting students to work cooperatively. It can be used in a wide variety of contexts, grade levels, and disciplines.

Cooperative learning is often cited as an effective intervention for many of the ills of our present day school system. It is promoted as an alternative to tracking and grouping, a way of mainstreaming academically handicapped students, a method of improving race relations, a means of increasing pro-social behavior, a solution to the problems of at-risk students, a technique of emphasizing and increasing higher order thinking skills, an alternative to special education, a process to prepare students for an increasingly collaborative work force, and as a method to increase the achievement of all students (Slavin 1989/90; Slavin 1991b).

Cooperative learning can help in many areas

But how effective is Cooperative Learning? Ellis and Fouts (1993) state that the empirical evidence accumulated from research studies in Cooperative Learning is staggering: there are numerous studies, reviews, syntheses, and meta-analysis, all of which conclude that Cooperative Learning is an effective strategy for raising student achievement. Ellis and Fouts cite four conclusions derived from this research.

1. The most successful approaches for enhancing student achievement include two key elements: group goals and individual accountability. Groups are rewarded based on the individual learning of all group members.

2. Its achievement effects are consistently positive when group goals and individual accountability are clear.

3. Its positive achievement effects have been found almost equally in all grade levels from 2 - 12 and in all major subjects, as well as rural, urban, and suburban schools and among high, average, and low achievers.

4. Its positive effects have been consistently documented as improving self-esteem, intergroup relations, acceptance of academically handicapped students, attitudes toward school, and the ability to work with others.

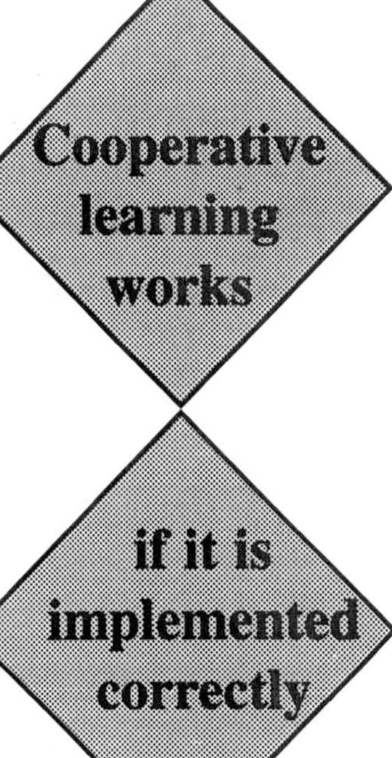

However, Slavin (1991b) as well as Sagor (1993) warn that unless Cooperative Learning is done properly it will create more difficulties for our at-risk students. The caution is that at-risk students risk further alienation if insufficient attention is paid to individual and group accountability. If the emphasis is placed on doing something instead of on learning something, low achievers will be seen as a hindrance rather than a help. For instance, if the group task is to complete a work sheet, there will be a great deal of answer sharing but very little explaining. According to Webb (1985), **the students who gain most from cooperative work are those who give and receive elaborated explanations.**

> **Extensive staff development in Cooperative Learning is essential for it to be effective**

Ellis and Fouts (1993) as well as Slavin (1989/90) also warn that in order for Cooperative Learning to actually accomplish these improvements, districts must invest in proper in-servicing of teachers. Ellis and Fouts state: " a brief introduction to such a complex idea is hardly sufficient" (p. 118). Slavin (1989/90) concurs: "Cooperative Learning can in fact accomplish this staggering array of objectives, but not as a result of a single three-hour in-service session" (p. 3).

Community Service Learning

Through the use of Cooperative Learning, students can learn that they are useful, contributing members of a class; however, through community service, they can learn that they are also useful, contributing members of a social community. The concept of youth community service is not a new one. Community Learning efforts have been on the national legislative agenda since the late Sixties and in the educational literature since the beginning of this century. John Dewey was an early proponent of the idea that learning should take place in real settings and directed toward meeting real community needs.

Harry Silcox (1993) feels strongly that "the twenty-first century requires a different vision of schools, and school-based community service must be considered one of the first and best solutions" (p. 58). Silcox, as well as Vandegrift and Sandler (1993), believe our schools and our nation must instill in our students a desire to be caring and contributing citizens who have a greater commitment to service. With the realization that government alone cannot solve all the problems in our communities and families, it becomes imperative that we raise caring individuals who can fill in the gap.

Proponents of community service learning cite many benefits for students and to the recipients of the service. What does the research have to say about the veracity of these claims? According to the Association for Supervision and Curriculum Development (ASCD, 1993), student service, combined with preparation and reflection, can promote academic learning and character development. They suggest that community service learning is a viable way to address a lack of tolerance and empathy for others in students. It gives students a vital way to make a difference in the lives of others.

Conrad and Hedin (1989), in a review of the research and programs, state that the findings are encouraging, though not without flaws. Because it is hard to define the independent variable of service and because there is a wide range of plausible outcomes of a given service, sound research into its effects are difficult but not impossible. The two types of research cited are both qualitative, including observations, self-reports, journals, interviews, and testimonials; and quantitative, including numbers derived from standardized instruments administered before and after service and then compared to control groups and subjected to a sophisticated statistical analysis.

Looking at quantitative research first, Conrad and Hedin (1989) state:

> Quantitative research into the impact of community service suggests that this approach can and often does have a positive impact on the intellectual and social-psychological development of participants.
>
> Researchers consistently report a heightened sense of personal and social responsibility, more positive attitudes towards adults and others, more active exploration of careers, enhanced self-esteem, growth in moral and ego development, more complex patterns of thought, and greater mastery of skills and content directly related to the experiences of participants.

> Furthermore, when the impact of service on others has been examined, youth have proven to be effective in raising math and reading scores and in reducing drug use among peers (p. 24).

Conrad and Hedin do caution, however, that due to methodological problems, a clear causal connection is difficult to make. They recommend that even though quantitative research is often considered "soft," in the area of community service it may be the most obvious and meaningful data of all. For example, the fact that participants are willingly and consistently acting in a socially responsible manner should be at least as relevant as a paper/pencil assessment of attitudes about being socially responsible. Consistent affirmation of the value of community service learning has been gathered from the available qualitative data, but the need for continued research on the subject is clear. Despite this, several authors still seem to accept that well-designed service programs can have a powerful impact on the social, psychological and intellectual development of students (Conrad and Hedin, 1989; Lockwood, 1990; Vandegrift and Sandler, 1993; Silcox, 1993).

Service learning is especially helpful for the at-risk student

According to Sagor (1993) and Vandegrift and Sandler (1993), community service is especially helpful for our at-risk students. Vandegrift and Sandler state that the reason for this is the fact that community service programs often include successful drop out prevention practices such as mentoring, tutoring, alternative programs and flexible scheduling, community and business collaboration, career counseling, and hands-on learning. Because these components are often central to service learning programs, they appear to offer a creative opportunity and viable strategy to reach at-risk students (Duckenfield and Swanson, 1992).

Heffernan and Tarlov (1989) state:

> Typically, disadvantaged youths are thought of as recipients of service, not givers. But such efforts can play an instrumental role in reducing the

> chance of dropping out of school or other poor outcomes among participants. Given proper guidance, direction, and supervision, young people respond well to the responsibility of service and sense the value of their efforts. This in turn increases youths' self-esteem and the likelihood of their becoming productive adults (p. 5).

Sagor (1993) also points to the fact that at-risk students often see themselves as victims. By becoming a service provider, the at-risk child can see him or herself as a protagonist who can take an active role to make things better for others as well as themselves.

Elements and Examples of Well Designed Community Service Programs

Sagor, 1993, believes that a quality service program would address the four basic psychological needs of usefulness, competency, belonging, and potency. Thus, children work to provide a valuable service directly for someone in need, contributing to their sense of *usefulness*. If this is on-going, children are more likely to feel a connection and a heightened sense of *belonging*. The work must be important so that those involved will feel a sense of *competence*, and thus after its accomplishment will lead to a sense of personal *potency*.

According to its advocates, a well-designed community service program should have several elements, some of which are listed here.

1 Proposals for specific projects should include (in as much detail as possible) how sites will be selected, how coordination and supervision will be achieved, how agencies and schools will communicate each other's expectations and responsibilities, and how students will be recruited, trained, supervised, evaluated, and provided opportunity for reflection (Silcox, 1993).

2 Projects should be an integral part of the educational program of the school, not just an add-on — there must be some type of measurable value obtained by the student (Silcox, 1993).

3 Opportunities for feedback and reflection are necessary for efficacy (Silcox, 1993).

4 Subject matter knowledge should not be the main goal, but learning to learn and applying subject matter embodied in the project in the daily lives of students. Teachers must become translators of information and knowledge that can be used in real-life situations, rather than someone who covers the regular curriculum (Silcox, 1993).

5 Quality programs must include professional and preprofessional training and practice for teachers. If staff members are reluctant or ill-prepared, service programs are not likely to be successful (Silcox, 1993).

The following is a list of some possible service learning strategies.

1. The entire school or individual classes adopt a community agency. Each student then spends the equivalent of one day per month providing volunteer work for that organization.

2. Students select their own service project, and then are expected to provide a minimum amount of service per school semester or year. This service could take place inside or outside the school community.

3. Community service is rewarded with school credit which may be either elective or required for a student to graduate.

4. Community service may be performed as a laboratory for an existing course or unit. For example, a home economics class may apply their decorating skills in the home of a low-income family.

5. A community service class may be offered which features a contrast between action and reflection. For example, a social studies class may meet only two days a week, with the remaining days spent in the community providing services.

6. Service can become a school wide or K-12 focus. In this model community, service permeates a school's total K-12 curriculum. Each academic department determines how the knowledge and skills of their discipline can be applied to benefit the community. This model also provides age-appropriate service opportunities on all levels.

Finally, community service learning may also benefit schools in their restructuring processes. Silcox (1990) believes that community service provides a viable means for restructuring our schools by forcing educators to focus on issues outside the school. This external focus allows schools more flexibility and creativity to adopt new programs that are relevant and meaningful for the student, and possibly encourages the community support that schools need to fund education.

Student Motivation

Discouraged learners often experience a sense of powerlessness over their lives and experiences. They tend to be externalizers, blaming their lack of success on others or bad luck. They sometimes fall into a victim role and exhibit "learned helplessness" tendencies. The following section takes a closer look at interventions which address these problems.

Tomlinson and Cross (1991) believe that school reform efforts over the past 30 to 40 years have overlooked a simple fact: student achievement gains must be accompanied by an increase in student effort. The authors conclude that students work below their potential only because they see no reason to do otherwise. Students are not excited by most of what is presented in schools, do not sense the value of it since by law they are required to attend, and are not pressed by cultural expectations to attain high standards.

Student excitement is facilitated by teacher excitement

According to Brophy and Good (1994), the degree to which students invest attention and effort in school depends on their motivation (their willingness to engage in school activities and their reasons for doing so). Brophy and Good also state that <u>a teacher's skill in motivating students to learn is key to his or her effectiveness</u>.

The following approaches to motivation theories fit into Feather's (1982) *Expectancy X Value* theory. This theory posits that the effort people are willing to expend on a task is a product of:

1. the degree to which they expect to be able to perform the task successfully if they apply themselves; and
2. the degree to which they value participation in the task itself or the benefits or rewards that successfully completing the task will bring.

One can not exist without the other. For example, students will not apply themselves if they expect to fail, even if they value the rewards; and conversely, will not apply themselves if they do not value the rewards, even if they are fairly certain they will succeed. Thus, it makes sense for teachers to be cognizant of helping students see the value of school activities, as well as to providing an environment of learning which will communicate to students their ability to achieve success if they apply the effort.

Four Preconditions for Successful use of Motivational Strategies:

Brophy and Good (1994) list four preconditions which need to be established for motivational strategies to be effective. They are:

Supportive Classrooms

1. **Supportive Environment:** Classrooms need to be orga nized in a supportive way, provide ample opportunities to learn, encourage student effort, be well-organized, have a relaxed and supportive atmosphere, focus on achieving mas tery, and emphasize individual progress rather than students comparisons.

2. **Appropriate Level of Challenge or Difficulty:** Tasks can not be so easy that they are busywork; nor can they be so difficult that students are unlikely to achieve success. Students

need to be paced through the curriculum as briskly as they can progress without unnecessary frustration. The level of difficulty is appropriate for students if they are clear about what to do and how to do it and, that they can achieve high levels of success if they are persistent and employ appropriate learning strategies. If this is a consistent pattern in class rooms, then students can concentrate on learning without worrying about failure.

Realistic Challenge

3. **Meaningful Learning Objectives:** Students are unlikely to want to engage in learning things which aren't worth learning. Skills which require a lot of practice are better exercised within whole-task application activities rather than isolated practice of part skills.

Relevance

4. **Moderation and Variation in Strategy Use:** It is important not to overuse motivational strategies. These strategies can be counterproductive if they are used when they are not needed, go on too long, are carried to extremes, or are used too routinely.

Overuse is a problem

Student Expectations for Success

Following the *Expectancy X Value* theory noted earlier, the following strategies and approaches relate to developing and maintaining student expectations of success. The following perceptions and attributes are listed by Brophy and Good (1994) as important for teachers to encourage and develop in their students: (pp.216-217)

6 attributes for student success

A. **Effort-outcome covariation:** Recognize that the amount of effort invested is directly related to the level of success that can be expected (Cooper, 1979).

B. **Internal locus of control:** Recognize that they control their own outcomes rather than being controlled by outside forces (Stipek & Weisz, 1981; Thomas, 1980).

C. **Concept of self as origin rather than pawn:** Recognize that it is through their own actions that they succeed rather than feeling directed by others and out of control of their own fate (deCharms, 1976).

D. **Sense of efficacy/competence:** Capable of succeeding if they put forth the necessary effort (Bandura, 1989; Bandura & Schunk, 1981; Schunk, 1991; Schunk & Hanson, 1985; Weisz & Cameron, 1985).

E. **Attribution to internal, controllable causes:** Success is attributed to ability and effort; and failure is attributed to lack of sufficient effort, use of inappropriate strategies, or lack of understanding of task directions (Butkowsky & Willows, 1980; Frieze, Francis, & Hanusa, 1983; Weiner, 1992; Whitley & Frieze, 1985).

F. **Incremental concept of ability:** Rather than being limited,our academic ability is developed as a result of the learn ing activities in which we participate (Dweck & Elliott,1983).

Goal Setting

Student goal setting is important

Because student reactions to their own performances are affected by their level of success as well as their perceptions of what they have achieved, it is important to help them value their accomplishments and to identify standards for judging them. Goal setting helps students to do this. According to Bandura (1986), goal setting plays an important role in the development of self-motivation by establishing a target or personal standard by which we can monitor and evaluate personal performance. Research also shows that setting goals and making a commitment to trying to reach these goals increases performance (Bandura & Schunk, 1981; Locke & Latham, 1990; Tollefson et al., 1984). Gaa (1973,1979) found that goal setting had a positive effect on elementary and secondary students. Goal setting is especially effective under the following circumstances:

Guidelines for goal setting

A. Goals are proximal rather than distal: Goals are related to tasks at hand rather than to an ultimate goal in the distant future. This is especially true for discouraged learners to avoid the feeling of being overwhelmed. Children with proximal goals performed better than those with distal or long-term goals, according to Bandura and Schunk (1981).

B. <u>Goals are specific rather than global:</u> For example, a student may set a goal of getting 8 of 10 spelling words correct on a test as opposed to "trying my best."

C. <u>Goals are challenging rather than too easy:</u> Goals should cause children to "stretch" from previous performances. However, the child must also believe he/she can accomplish the goal.

Guidelines for goal setting

Brophy and Good (1994) offer several specific suggestions for student goal setting. When students are given a page of math problems and told to "do as many as they can," the order is too vague to function as a specific challenge. It would be better to ask students to adopt the goal of solving each problem and persisting until they are confident that a specified number of problems were done correctly. Students would then be more likely to use higher quality problem-solving efforts and persistence. If assignments are brief, successful attainment of the instructional goal may be an appropriate goal in itself. If the assignment is large or long, it is important to establish step-by-step goals which lead to the achievement of the total assignment (Bandura & Schunk, 1981).

Teachers need to help students form challenging but reachable goals and develop goal commitment. Students must take the goals seriously and be committed to trying to reach them. Teachers need to provide encouragement and support to students, which will assist in the development of the commitment to accomplishing the goal.

Students must experience success.

Good and Brophy (1994), having reviewed multiple sources of research in this area, provide the reader with a variety of possible strategies useful in developing in students a link between their effort and the outcome.

Modeling: Teachers can model effort-outcome linkages by thinking out loud when demonstrating tasks, by exhibiting persistent effort, and by searching for better strategies when they encounter frustration or failure (Zimmerman & Blotner, 1979).

Socialization and Feedback: Teachers must develop the culture in the classroom that all students can succeed if they put forth effort and are persistent. Teachers must also work to develop the students' confidence in their ability to be successful by encouraging and supporting them. In addition, teachers cause students to focus on their own academic growth as opposed to comparing themselves to others.

Portray Effort as Investment Rather Than Risk: Students must learn that the process of learning is risky, frustrating and confusing at times, for everyone. Persistence and effort at these times, along with realistic goals, will result in academic success.

Skill Development Portrayed as Incremental and Domain Specific: Teachers need to demonstrate to students how their academic abilities have changed and grown over the years. Also, teachers need to show students that some have strengths in one subject and others strength in another.

Focus on Mastery: The goal is mastery. To accomplish this goal, continual monitoring, analysis and feedback are essential. Teachers must encourage persistence and provide additional instruction, practice opportunities, and time for students to be successful.

Teach these to students

Good and Brophy point out that discouraged students may benefit from attributional retraining. These approaches use modeling, socialization, practice, and feedback to teach students to

1. Concentrate on the task at hand rather than worry about failure.

2. Cope with failure by retracing their steps to find their mis take or by analyzing the problem to find another approach rather than giving up.

3. Attribute their failures to insufficient effort, lack of information, or use of ineffective strategies rather than lack of ability (Craske, 1988; Dweck & Elliott, 1983; Fowler & Peterson, 1981; Medway & Venino, 1982).

According to Alderman (1990), it is the teacher's role to help students make the appropriate attribution through feedback given about why the students succeeded or failed at the task. Asking students "What did you do when you tried?" helps them focus on the kinds of effort they employed.

Influencing Students to Value Academic Activities

The second part of the *Expectancy X Value* theory of motivation relates to the degree to which students value school learning. It pertains both to the benefits students believe they will gain and to the reasons they may engage in learning in the first place. Students can be motivated extrinsically or intrinsically. If their only reason for doing an activity is to get something outside the activity itself, then the motivation is extrinsic. If the person would do the activity anyway, even if there was no reward or punishment involved, then they are intrinsically motivated. An experience is described as autotelic if it is enjoyable in and of itself.

Extrinsic & Intrinsic Motivation

Ames and Ames (1989) feel that in our everyday lives we are often motivated by varying mixtures of extrinsic and intrinsic rewards. The best case scenario is when a person's activities are simultaneously autotelic and productive. People then feel that what they do is worth doing for its own sake, is not a waste of time, and will be productive in both the present and future. How do we combine intrinsic rewards with activities that are useful in the long run? The following section will discuss the advantages and disadvantages of extrinsic and intrinsic motivational strategies.

Using Extrinsic Motivation to Help Students Value School Experiences

Discouraged students often need extrinsic rewards

Unfortunately, as noted by several researchers (Slavin, 1991b; Graves, 1991), a majority of tasks expected of students in school settings are not ones students would normally be motivated to do on their own. Additionally, discouraged students will be even less likely to be motivated to participate in tasks they have repeatedly failed at in the past. According to Brophy and Good

(1994), extrinsic motivation strategies are, in some ways, the simplest, most direct, and most adaptable of the methods for encouraging students to value school learning.

Arguments against the use of extrinsic rewards

Opponents of extrinsic motivational strategies list the following arguments against their use:

1. Task engagement quality and achievement is higher when students perceive themselves to be engaged in a task for their own reasons, rather than to please an authority figure, gain a reward, or escape a punishment (Deci & Ryan, 1985; Lepper, 1983)
2. Students will concentrate more on meeting minimum standards for performance rather than on doing high-quality work if they perceive that they are performing a task solely to obtain a reward (Condry & Chambers, 1978; Kruglanski, 1978)
3. In team competitions losing team members may devalue one another and scapegoat the individuals they hold responsible for the loss (Ames, 1984; Johnson & Johnson, 1985)
4. Extrinsic inducements may reduce creativity, encourage students to work quickly, take few risks, and focus narrowly on a task (Amabile, 1983)
5. Grades and some forms of praise can undermine interest in an activity (Ryan, 1982; Butler, 1987);
6. Extrinsic rewards undermine intrinsic motivation (Kohn, 1990; Kohn, 1991).

In support of extrinsic rewards

Contrasting opinions are also found. Following are some of the findings and arguments from those supporting extrinsic rewards:

1. The evidence that extrinsic rewards undermine intrinsic motivation is mixed and subject to alternative interpretations (Graves, 1991)
2. The positive effects of Cooperative Learning on student achievement depends on the use of group rewards based on the individual learning of group members (Slavin, 1988, 89/90, 90a; Newmann and Thompson, 1987; Davidson, 1985)

3. There are as many studies demonstrating that rewards enhance continuing motivation or that they have no effect on continuing motivation as they are showing that it undermines motivation (Slavin, 1991b)
4. Studies showing a negative effect on intrinsic interest involved a short time period, an artificial setting, and involved a task unlike most school tasks (Slavin, 1991b)
5. There are consistent findings that rewards increase motivation when the task involved is one that students would not do on their own without rewards (Bates, 1979; Morgan, 1984; Lepper and Greene, 1978)

6. Rewards, given over a period of days or weeks, do not diminish intrinsic motivation (Vasta et al., 1978)
7. Rewards enhance intrinsic motivation if they convey information on performance relative to others (Boggiano et al., 1982), or if they are social rather than tangible (Lepper and Greene, 1978; Deci and Ryan, 1985).

Graves (1991,p.78) lists the conditions under which extrinsic rewards appear to have their most damaging effects on intrinsic motivation:

1. When students would be willing to engage in the activities without the use of rewards.
2. When the rewards may be seen by students as an attempt to manipulate and control their behavior.

Extrinsic rewards are the least damaging to intrinsic motivation, and may actually enhance it, under the following conditions:

Extrinsic rewards are the least damaging under these conditions

1. When the tasks are ones students would be unwilling to do on their own.
2. When the rewards are largely symbolic in form, serving more to communicate to students how well they are doing and their teacher's pride in their accomplishments, than as "payment" for their performance.
3. When the rewards are social rather than tangible.
4. When the rewards are unanticipated.

Good and Brophy (1994) give the following cautions and guidlines for the use of extrinsic rewards:

> Rewards are more effective for increasing effort than for improving quality of performance. They guide behavior more effectively when there is a clear goal and a clear strategy to follow than when goals are more ambiguous or when students must discover or invent new strategies rather than merely activate familiar ones. Thus, rewards are better used with boring or unpleasant tasks than with attractive or interesting ones, better with routine tasks than with novel ones, better with specific intentional learning tasks than with incidental learning or discovery tasks, and better with tasks where speed or performance or quantity of output is of more concern than creativity, artistry, or craftsmanship. It is better to offer rewards as incentives for meeting performance standards on skills that require a great deal of drill and practice than it is for work on a major research or demonstration project. (p. 225).

Appropriate uses of competition

Competition, when handled appropriately, can add excitement and student motivation to class learning activities. Good and Brophy (1994) suggest that competition can be individual or group but must follow some basic guidelines to be successful. These guidelines are:

1. It may be counterproductive in some situations to add another competitive element to an already competitive grading situation.
2. Competition can be distracting, so it is important to it by emphasizing the content learned not the winners and losers.
3. Competition is more appropriate with routine practice tasks than with creative or discovery tasks.
4. Everyone must have an equal chance of winning. Teachers must pay careful attention to how teams are formed. Also teachers should have children compare the themselves to previous results.

5. Since competition creates losers as well as winners, teachers should minimize the risk by determining winners primarily through degree of effort (and some luck) rather than by ability, and pay more attention to whole class accomplishments rather than who won.

Developing Intrinsic Motivation to Help Students Value School Experiences

Research on characteristics of tasks that people tend to find intrinsically rewarding (Deci & Ryan, 1985; Lepper & Greene, 1978; Malone & Lepper, 1987) are describe as those that:

1. maximize free choice and autonomy;
2. are free of pressures or risks.

These characteristics are contrary to many school activities where students are required to receive instruction in a prescribed curriculum and to be graded by an authority figure (the teacher) on their academic performance.

Good and Brophy (1994) state that, although it may be difficult to take advantage of students' existing intrinsic motivation because of the above factors, there are some common elements that help make classroom activities enjoyable and intrinsically rewarding for most students. Following is a description of these elements which promote intrinsic motivation.

1 **Active Participation**: Active participation is when students interact with and manipulate information, materials and ideas. Lecture and most worksheets are not considered active participation. Students must experience realistic application and problem solving activities. They can actively participate when involved with experiments, role-plays, simulations, lab work, debates and research projects.

strategies for intrinsic student motivation

2 **Higher-Level Objectives and Divergent Questions:** Students must be urged to function at the application, analysis, synthesis and evaluation level of Bloom's Taxonomy. To accomplish this teachers need to implement strategies as described above in "Active Participation." such as stimulating students to think creatively about problems,

HOW MUCH OF THIS IS HAPPENING IN YOUR BUILDING?

discuss and debate issues, and explore cause and effect relationships. In addition, teachers must continually be asking students the following two questions: "How do you know you have the correct answer?" and "What process did you use to get the answer?" By having the students respond to these questions, the teacher causes the students to think at higher levels. After asking these questions and before saying whether a student has answered correctly or not, the teacher should ask the other students to signal whether they agree, disagree, or are unsure of the answer given. This can cause discussions with divergence of fact and opinion.

3 **Feedback Features:** Students like feedback to see how they are doing in the eyes of the teacher. In addition, they should be encouraged and taught to do self-assessment. The more immediate the feedback, the more likely the student will be motivated to continue the behavior. Teachers can facilitate this by explaining clearly the performance criteria and modeling how the task should be done. Students then use the criteria to assess themselves and others. Teachers must continually monitor and give students feedback.

WHAT IS BEING DONE TO MAKE LEARNING FUN

4 **Incorporating Game-Like Features into Activities:** Children love games and play them continually. We must build on this idea during the teaching/learning process. The more teachers can incorporate the following ideas, the more motivated the children become to learn. Children enjoy problem solving, avoiding traps, being detectives, solving puzzles, creating games or puzzles for others to do, and even creating questions (and the answers) for tests. These activities are effective only if they have clear objectives and are challenging to students.

Create Emotional H¿¿ks

5 **Opportunities for Students to Create Finished Products:** When students have the opportunity to display a finished product, motivation often improves. Science and social studies projects and book reports are the most common, however, allowing children to take ownership can add challenge and interest to any area. Children enjoy putting poetry to music (rap) or reading in a rhythmic pattern while doing double dutch jump rope.

6 **Inclusion of Simulation Elements:** Children have rich imaginations and enjoy using them. Teachers can use this concept by having children simulate, role play, or analyze what it would be like to be in a particular situation or event. By doing this students learn the important concepts and also are more likely to retain them.

7 **Opportunities for Peer Interaction:** Most students enjoy the opportunity to interact with their peers. However, for this to be effective these interactions must have a clear instructional objective. In addition, students working in pairs, trios or quartets can be more actively involved than in whole class discussions or activities, as each student can have a substantive role to play. The combination of this peer interaction with other ideas presented in this section can create a powerful motivational force in the classroom.

THIS IS SUPPORTED BY COOPERATIVE LEARNING RESEARCH

8 **Project-Based Learning:** This approach described by Blumenfeld et al. (1991) focuses on long term projects which integrate many subjects as students work to accomplish the project. Good and Brophy describe it as follows: "Within this framework, students pursue solutions to authentic problems by asking and refining questions, debating ideas, making predictions, designing plans or experiments, collecting and analyzing data, drawing conclusions, communicating their ideas and findings to others, asking new questions, and creating products." (232-233.) For example, a fifth grade class planned and implemented a Young Author's Conference at a local hotel for 1500 elementary students.

PROJECTS MUST BE INTERESTING AND WORTH WHILE TO THE STUDENTS

Developing in Students a Motivation to Learn

As educators we must create the situation where children are attracted to and interested in learning, and where they find academic activities of value and want to participate. Even the most apathetic student will show a desire to learn if the teacher is able to spark his/her interest In addition to sparkin interest, educators must also teach children how to learn.

15 ways to motivate students

The following strategies (Brophy and Good, 1994) focus on ways teachers can spark student interest, as well as help students gain some insight into how they learn.

1. Teacher Modeling of Motivation to Learn

Educators must model motivation to learn if they expect students to be motivated to learn. This can be accomplished by demonstrating enthusiasm, curiosity, excitement, and wonder at what you see, hear or do. Also, it is important to model a willingness to take on new or unusual tasks and how to work through unexpected problems. When educators model these things, students see people who find learning motivating and fun.

2. Communicating Desirable Expectations and Attributions

When teachers treat students as if they are eager learners, students are more likely to become exactly that.

Communicating that you believe the students are capable and enthusiastic learners is far more likely to cause students to put effort forth than if the educator communicates that he/she believes students are not capable. We have a tendency to live up to the expectations others have of us.

How are mistakes handled in your classroom?

3. Minimize Performance Anxiety

Structuring most classroom activities as learning experiences rather than as tests will minimize anxiety over performance. Teachers must do summative evaluations eventually, but the bulk of the classroom experience should be focused on making progress and learning from our mistakes.

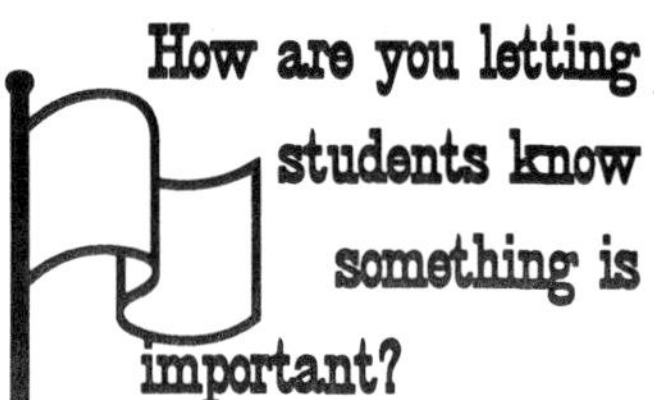

4. Project Intensity

Teachers should cue students that particular material is important and deserves close attention. Intensity is projected primarily through body language and voice intonation.

5. Project Enthusiasm

Enthusiasm is often contagious. If the teacher is excited about the lesson, the students are much more likely to be enthusiastic. With an enthusiastic presentation by the teacher, students are more likely to value the topic or activity.

6. Induce Task Interest or Appreciation

Teachers can induce appreciation for a topic by making connections with the students' prior knowledge or creating relevance by showing students how the topic/skills can be applied in a meaningful way in their lives.

7. etaerC ytisoiruC ro esnepsuS

Teachers can create curiosity and suspense by doing something in a unique or novel way or by posing questions that make students want to "figure it out." This can be as simple as writing words backwards as you see above. Also, by using fonts on computers named "Wingdings" or "Dingbats," teachers can create codes which students must break. Another way is to use a strategy such as "KWL" where the students tell what they know about a topic and what they would like to learn. The "facts" that they know and the questions they want to learn can be used by the teacher to create curiosity.

8. Make Abstract Content More Personal, Concrete, or Familiar

Theories, principles and definitions are frequently abstract and meaningless to students. To make content concrete, teachers must connect the new learning to student prior knowledge. Also, concepts become more concrete when teachers use analogies, metaphors, personal stories, demonstrations and simulations to illustrate content.

9. Induce Dissonance or Cognitive Conflict

There is much we can do to cause students to wonder about something. Take two ideas which appear to conflict with each other and show how they are the same, then ask the question, "How can that be?" Teachers may also purposely pose questions where the teacher knows the students have a difference of opinion.

How can that be?

10. Induce Students to Generate Their Own Motivation to Learn

One way to encourage students to identify what they want to learn about a topic is to pose 3 - 5 questions which can be answered true/false. After the students have answered, they must find information in the text, video or lecture to support their answer. Doing this in pairs and telling the two students they must agree on both the answer (true/false) as well as the support information is also motivating.

11. State Learning Objectives and Provide Advance Organizers

Motivation to learn is greater when students have an organizational structure to which they can connect the concepts to be learned. This must begin with the students' prior knowledge of the topic. The statement of the objective at the beginning of the lesson, along with the use of advanced organizers or graphic organizers, can be a powerful tools for teachers to motivate students.

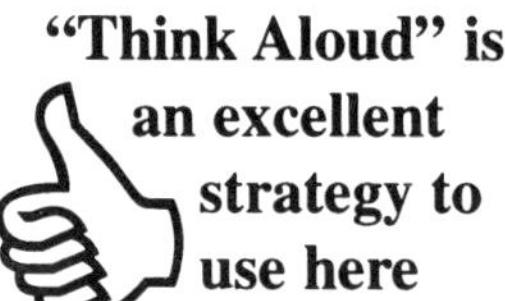

12. Model and Induce Metacognitive Awareness of Learning Strategies

Teachers must model and teach students to think and analyze. This is most commonly done when an elementary teacher is teaching how to add two columns of numbers with carrying. The teacher usually talks through each step so the students understand the mental process to be used. The more the teachers can cause students to use this process, the more likely the students will be successful and motivated.

13. Actively Preparing to Learn

Frequently students have not been taught the important cognative skills to prepare themselves to learn. These include activating their prior knowledge about the topic, clarifying the objective of the lesson, previewing the tasks, and establishing a systematic process to follow. Affective skills are also important, including learning how to concentrate, focusing on progress being made, and persistence.

14. Committing Material to Memory

Teachers can teach students techniques for remembering efficiently. Mnemonics are powerful strategies. Also, strategies such as paraphrasing and summarizing information into their own words, relating it to what they already know, and assessing their understanding through questions are useful for helping students retain the substance of the material.

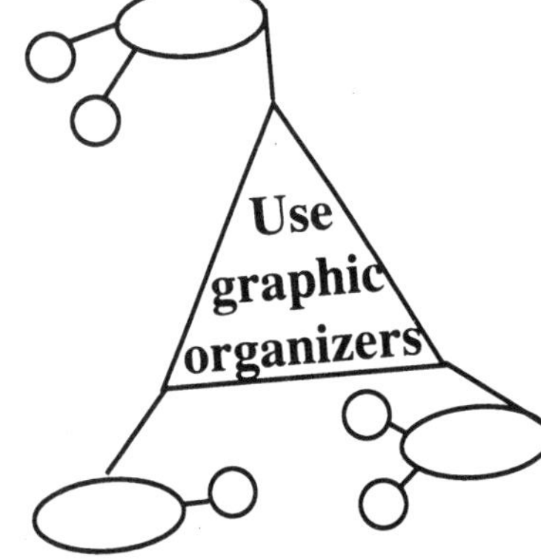

15. Organizing and Structuring the Content

Teaching students how to categorize material facilitates their learning and is motivational. Graphic organizers, semantic maps, Frayer model, chapter mapping, and Venn diagram are powerful tools in this regard. Graphically "outlining" helps the brain to "chunk" and to "make sense" of things.

Discipline

As noted earlier, at-risk students frequently exhibit behavioral problems. According to Skiba, McLeskey, Waldron, & Grizzle (1993) at-risk students exhibit more inappropriate behaviors and participate less in academically engaged time. Not surprisingly, there is also a cause-and-effect relationship between misbehavior and poor school achievement. **Misbehavior has been demonstrated to predicate a drop in both grades and achievement, while, conversely, low grades also lead to greater misbehavior (Myers et al., 1987).** The importance of examining school discipline policies is stated effectively by Moles (1990):

> By its effects on teachers, the school learning environment, and individual students, misbehavior can have a profound influence on student achievement. It should be clear that an improvement in student behavior could reap large benefits for learning (p. 5).

Schools have control over many factors that significantly influence both the achievement and behavior of students. In their studies of high schools experiencing different numbers of discipline problems, Wayson and Pinnel (1982) point out that that:

> When discipline problems occur in school, they can more often be traced to dysfunction in the interpersonal climate and organizational patterns of the school than to malfunctions in the individual. In short, misbehaving students are often reacting in a predictable and even sensible way to the school as it affects them and as they have learned to perceive it and react to it (p. 9).

Discipline problems are always symptomatic of other problems

School discipline touches on many aspects of the school environment. It is the opinion of several researchers (Short, Short, & Blanton, 1994; Moles, 1990; Duke, 1990) that discipline should be conceived as an organizational issue. <u>Techniques for dealing with discipline problems are important, but focusing solely on</u>

these neglects the importance of personal and organizational characteristics. Short et al (1994) describe some of the problems of a narrow focus on strategies:

Important

> Emphasizing technique, we firmly believe, is a narrow and potentially dangerous solution for school discipline . . . When techniques fail, and we know that they sometimes do, educators often simply intensify their efforts, or they look for another, similar technique. By replacing unsuccessful techniques with new techniques, other potential problems and solutions within the school environment are ignored. These solutions implicitly identify teachers or students as problems, and technique as the solution. We have seen simplistic analysis of characteristics and needs of individual schools, resulting in little real change in the level of discipline problems (pp. 5-6).

The following three topics will be discussed in this section as they relate to school discipline: school climate, effective teaching and classroom management, and possible intervention strategies. The first two are prevention related, while the last deals exclusively with interventions.

School Climate

Smey-Richman's (1991) research indicates that school culture and social systems are important areas of school climate on which to focus.

Organizational factors which increase student achievement

School effectiveness research offers insight into organizational factors which are present in schools with relatively high levels of student achievement. Duke (1990) lists some of these as:

1. Frequent and systematic evaluation of students, goals linked to the acquisition of basic skills, and clear rules for student conduct are used (Stedman, 1985)
2. Effective schools exhibit cultural norms which include staff collegiality and a pervasive caring for students (Anderson 1985)
3. Fluid ability grouping strategies are used, minimizing student tracking (Stedman, 1985).

Duke (1990) summarizes his findings from an extensive review of school organizational factors:

> In summary, what is known about the organization of orderly schools is that they are characterized by a commitment to appropriate student behavior and clear behavioral expectations for students. Rules, sanctions, and procedures are discussed, debated, and frequently formalized into school discipline and classroom management plans. To balance this emphasis on formal procedure, the climate in these organizations conveys concern for students as individuals. This concern manifests itself in a variety of ways, including efforts to involve students in school decision making, school goals that recognize multiple forms of student achievement, and a de-emphasis on homogeneous grouping (p. 44).

Are these things happening in your building?

School climate research solidly substantiates the importance of climate for student achievement (Agnew, 1981; Anderson, 1982; Brookover et al., 1977; Heck et al., 1990; Howe, 1985; Keefe et al. 1985; Lezotte et al, 1980; Stickard and Mayberry, 1986; and Stronge and Jones, 1991). Bulach and Malone (1994), quote from Hoyle, English, and Steffy (1985):

> School climate may be one of the most important ingredients of a successful instructional program. Without a climate that creates a harmonious and well functioning school, a high degree of academic achievement is difficult, if not downright impossible to obtain (p. 15).

Short et al. (1994) sum up well the importance of school climate:

> We have found that school practices that heighten student and staff involvement may decrease the occurrence of discipline problems. Student participation in school activities strongly relates to student commitment to schools. Activities that increase status, visibility, recognition, and group cohesiveness may decrease student alienation. Students want to be a part of schools that solicit

> their involvement and input. Negative student behaviors seem to decrease in schools in which the faculty have created senses of student belonging and involvement (p. 8)

Effective Teachers and Classroom Management

Effectively run classrooms occur as a result of the organizational and management skills of the teacher. A study done by Kounin and colleagues (1970) compared the differences between how effective and ineffective classroom managers were behaving prior to student disruptions. A study done by Brophy and Evertson (1976) further supported Kounin's findings, discovering that effective teachers exhibited specific behaviors which prevented disruption and facilitated learning. In 1980, studies conducted by Emmer, Evertson, and Anderson indicated that classrooms which ran smoothly throughout the school year were a result of effective planning and organization implemented during the first few weeks of school. Specifically, effective classroom teachers:

What the teacher does in the first few weeks of school is critical to effective discipline

1. Provided students with clear instruction in desirable classroom behavior.
2. Carefully monitored students' performance.
3. Took time to re-teach behaviors that were not mastered.

Since these early findings, there has been a multitude of research substantiating the correlation between effective classroom management and student behaviors. These studies offer teachers a coherent set of principles to follow (Brophy, 1983, 1988; Doyle, 1986; Emmer & Aussiker, 1990; Evertson & Harris, 1992; Gettinger, 1988; McCaslin & Good, 1992).

In a review of these findings, Good & Brophy (1994) state that:

> The findings converge on the conclusion that teachers who approach classroom management as a process of establishing and maintaining effective learning environments tend to be more successful than teachers who place more emphasis on their roles as authority figures or disciplinarians (p. 129).

In summarizing the research, Good and Brophy also found that the keys to successful management are proactivity and clear communication of expectation. A proactive approach includes the following characteristics:

1. The focus is preventive rather than reactive,
2. Management methods which encourage appropriate student conduct are integrated with instructional methods that encourage student achievement,
3. The focus is also on managing the class as a group rather than on changing the behavior of individual students.

Teachers must be proactive

Good and Brophy contend that a teacher must have certain key attitudes to be successful, which they list as:

Teacher attitude

- Teachers must like their students and respect them as individuals. This appreciation and concern will come through in their tone of voice, facial expressions, and everyday behavior. In return, the students will like and respect the teacher.

- Teachers must be interested in getting to know their students individually.

- Teachers must establish credibility early and maintain it throughout the year. This means establishing fair rules and consistently enforcing them.

- Teachers must assume responsibility for seeing that their students learn.

How prevalent is this in your school?

- Teachers must value and enjoy learning and expect students to do the same.

Other general principles of effectively managed classrooms, taken from the research by Good and Brophy (1994), are listed below.

1. Plan rules (general expectations) and procedures (methods for daily routines) in advance. Behavioral rules need to be kept to a minimum and clearly stated along with rationale for their use. **Often, demonstrations are needed, with an opportunity provided for students to practice.** Every year students are required to take on new responsibilities and experiences, and, because of this, **they need clear direction on the "how-tos."**

2. Allow students to assume responsibilities whenever possible. The relationship between student and teacher should be a cooperative one, allowing students to voice concerns and encouraging them to take more responsibility.

3. Minimize disruptions and delays. This means avoiding situations where students are forced to wait idly. Preparing teaching materials ahead of time, organizing supplies, and arranging for smooth transitions in the classroom are helpful techniques to avoid delays.

Boring **seat work leads to bored and disruptive students**

4. Plan independent activities as well as organized lessons. Seat work should be a basic part of the curriculum rather than busywork; therefore, it needs to be planned just as carefully as lessons are. If students understand its importance, are held accountable for the work, and are monitored in their progress, boredom, and unclear expectations can be avoided.

If students are motivated and actively engaged in classroom activities, discipline problems will be minimal. When teachers use "best practice" student motivation often improves and discipline problems are reduced. See the book by Zemelman, Daniels, and Hyde (1993), Best Practice in Teaching, which lists these best practices in mathematics, reading, science, social studies, and writing.

Interventions When Discipline Problems Occur

Although many behavioral problems can be prevented through the use of the techniques described in the previous section, discipline problems will still occur in classrooms, especially with at-risk students. Following is a review of interventions used when discipline problems occur in the classroom.

Punishment

Punitive responses are often the intervention of choice in our schools. Punitive responses include the use of sarcasm, yelling, verbal threats, revocation of privileges, extra work, time-out, cor poral punishment, detention, suspension, and expulsion. With regards to punishment, Good and Brophy (1994) write:

> A great body of evidence (reviewed in Bandura, 1986, 1989) shows that punishment can control misbehavior, but by itself it will not teach desirable behavior or even reduce the desire to misbehave. Thus, punishment is never a solution by itself; it can only be part of a solution (p. 176).

Punishment is never a solution by itself. . . It can only be part of a solution

Jones and Jones (1995) cite several other problems with punishment. The first of these is that punishment does not teach students alternative methods of behavior so they can avoid behavior problems in the future. Punishment appears to inhibit both students' learning (Englander, 1986) and their appreciation of learning, as well as causing an increase in aggression (Kounin, 1970; Kounin & Gump, 1961). In a review of studies in which students were found to learn the most effectively (Mortimore & Sammons, 1987; Rutter, Maughan, Mortimore, Ouston, & Smith, 1979), researchers found high rates of positive reinforcement and lower rates of punishment.

Research also disproves the belief that punishment is successful in changing student behavior. Emmer and Aussiker (1987) examined the literature to determine the effectiveness of four discipline approaches: teacher effectiveness training, reality therapy, assertive discipline and Adlerian-based approaches. They found that many more studies documented little improvement in student behavior when using assertive discipline than studies that documented improved behavior through its use. Becker, Engelmann, and Thomas (1975) found that misbehavior in the classroom increased from 9% to 31% when teachers were asked to increase their use of punitive control methods.

Misbehavior increased 9 -31% when teachers increased use of punitive control methods

Punishment also gives students a reason to blame others rather than to accept personal responsibility for their actions. According to Glasser (1988), 95% of all student discipline problems are caused by student frustration with being unable to fulfill their basic psychological need for power. Their misbehavior is often an attempt to gain this sense of power or control in their lives. Slavin (1986) found that punishment must be applied consistently, or it will increase resentment and de-emphasize desired behavior. Jones and Jones (1995) also state that, rather than solving a problem, the use of punishments such as writing sentences or assigning additional homework can cause students to become aversive to these activities, which work to defeat the overall purpose of the entire learning process.

Many authors argue that punishment should not be considered as the central means of solving discipline problems (Doyle, 1990; Emmer and Aussiker, 1990; Wynne, 1990. Moles (1990) states that it does have a role in reducing student misbehavior and that <u>one of the best-established research findings is the link between firm, fairly administered, and consistent discipline and lower levels of discipline problems in schools</u> (Metz, 1978; Gottfredson and Gottfredson, 1985; National Institute of Education, 1978).

No discussion of punishment is complete without considering suspension programs. Despite its widespread use, there are few well-designed studies of suspension (Toby & Scrupski, 1990). In order to avoid giving suspended students the freedom they may actually be wishing for, many schools have moved towards in-school suspension programs. Listed below are the three types of in-school programs described by Short, Short and Blanton (1994).

> **Punitive** These programs expect students to complete classwork, often without help, while serving a required amount of punishment time. This model includes restrictive rules and coercive strategies, and <u>operates on the belief that the problem lays with the students.</u>
>
> **Therapeutic** These programs incorporate activities that help students improve self-esteem and communication skills, successfully complete classwork, participate in decision making, and develop coping techniques for dealing with the school environment. This approach utilizes a variety of counseling approaches, including individual and group/peer counseling, reality therapy, and referrals to outside counseling services. There may also be activities in staff development, parental training, home and school survival skills for students, as well as a time-out room (Short, 1988).

Academic These programs are based on the theoretical orientation that discipline problems evolve from a student's frustration with learning difficulties. Emphasis is placed on basic skills in reading and writing, study habits, and other academic skills. If a student is in need of individual instruction, a teacher is available to provide it. It is a structured experience with goal-oriented rules and regulations (Short, 1988).

In-school programs may combine different theoretical orientations or center around just one. Many articles cite success when describing particular programs (Sykora, 1981); however, Toby and Scrupski (1990) state that comprehensive research into in-school suspension programs is rare and sometimes of dubious quality. Many articles citing success are written by individual administrators who may be biased towards their own particular programs (Short et al, 1994). According to Mizell (1979), in-school suspension programs, although popular, are not likely to lead to changed behavior in most situations. Remediating the situation and teaching the student self-discipline should be the ultimate goal, rather than viewing the student as the problem and removing him or her from school (Sabatino, 1983; Short et al, 1994).

In-school suspension programs are not likely to change behavior

In a study that analyzed national level data gathered for the Safe School Study, Wu, Pink, Crain, & Moles (1982) found that the critical school variables which influenced suspension of students were teacher judgments and attitudes, school management and student governance practices, and the racial, socioeconomic, and academic bias present in the school. These researchers suggest that a student's chances of being suspended are increased if:

1. Teachers are seen by students as relatively uninterested in their lives.
2. Teachers believe students are incapable of solving problems.
3. Disciplinary matters are handled largely by administrative rules.
4. The school is unable to provide consistent and fair governance.
5. There is a relatively high degree of academic bias among school personnel.

Factors which increase student's chance of getting suspended

6. There is a relatively high degree of racial bias present in the school (271).

How does this compare to data for your school?

Short et al (1994) cite some disturbing statistics from the study done by Wu et al (1982). Specifically, these are that:

1. "Males were more likely to be suspended than females;
2. Blacks were twice as likely to be suspended than whites;
3. Students whose fathers did not work or who received free lunch were more likely to be suspended than those who did not receive free lunch;
4. Students' chances of suspension were increased by a poor academic record or low ability level." (p. 23)

Critical Questions About In-School Suspension

Short, Short and Bland (1994) offer a list of critical questions schools should discuss when using in-school suspension programs. They are listed below:

Questions worth careful consideration

1. What do school personnel hope to accomplish through the in-school suspension program?
2. Is there a total school discipline program? What does in-school suspension accomplish in the total discipline program?
3. What perceptions and philosophies are predominantly held by school staff members: Are they mostly punitive in nature?
4. Is there an attempt to identify the reasons for rules, infractions and misbehaviors? There may well be more effective strategies for curbing incidents of class skipping, truancy, and many others.
5. Does the discipline program provide positive reinforcers? Is discipline defined only in terms of punishment?
6. Students who get into trouble are not a homogeneous group. Would the school be more successful in changing student behaviors if they used in-school suspension for only the most troublesome group of disrupters and developed other strategies for all other nonviolent disruption acts?

7. Is student behavior changed when they are suspended for a specified period of time? Does it encourage the "passive waiting out" of time?
8. Is the in-school suspension program evaluated using a valid measure?

Alternative Methods of Dealing with Discipline Problems

Schools need to look closely at their use of punishment techniques, especially for at-risk students, who can easily become unmotivated and psychologically disengaged from school. If punishment should not be used as the central means of handling discipline problems, and if the identification and remediation of the problem is the ultimate goal, what interventions are likely to accomplish this task? Various researchers have developed theoretical perspectives which help us to understand and influence children's school behavior. A few of these perspectives are listed here.

Glasser's Reality Therapy, Control Theory, and The Quality School

In Reality Therapy and Schools Without Failure (1965, 1969), William Glasser described a simple and effective method of helping children solve problems and change behavior. In this approach, the teacher attempts to help students see that their current behavior is keeping them from reaching their goals, and offers to help them find better ways to achieve those goals. His seven steps to effective discipline are cited by Jones and Jones (1995):

1. Be warm, personal and willing to become emotionally involved.
2. Deal with specific, current behavior.
3. Help the student make a value judgment about his or her behavior.
4. Work out a plan for changing the behavior.
5. Receive a commitment from the student to carry out the plan.

Glasser's 7 steps to effective discipline

6. Follow up by checking to see how the plan is working.
7. Do not punish the student by being negative or sarcastic, and do not accept excuses if inappropriate behavior continues.

This type of problem-solving technique gives students a sense of power over their situation. Additionally, it can also help to correct the problem, something which does not usually occur with traditional time-out punishments. Glasser believes that many of the discipline problems in school are caused because basic student needs are not being fulfilled.

Research on Glasser's work has produced mixed but generally positive results Emmer & Aussiker, 1987). Although Good and Brophy (1994) state that there is little systematic research available on Glasser's theories, they feel that the general principles underlying them are supported by Brophy and McCaslin's (1992) research examining various strategies for coping with chronic personality and behavioral problems.

Gordon's Teacher Effectiveness Training

Thomas Gordon, author of the Teacher Effectiveness Training (1974), advocated a "no lose" approach to resolving conflicts. Gordon trains teachers to recognize problem ownership. Teachers are asked to reflect is the problem theirs or the students? If the problem is the student's, teachers should use empathy and active listening skills, which involve reflective listening techniques. If the problem is the teacher's, "I" messages should be used to help students recognize the problem behavior and its effects on others. Conflicts are resolved through the following six-step, "no lose" method for finding a solution which satisfies all parties:

Gordon's 6 step process

1. Define the problem,
2. Generate possible solutions,
3. Evaluate those solutions,
4. Decide which is the best,
5. Determine how to implement that solution,
6. Assess the effectiveness of the solution after implementation. If it isn't working well, a new agreement is negotiated.

As with Glasser, the research supporting Gordon's strategy is mixed, but generally positive (Emmer & Aussiker, 1987).

In a discussion of the use of problem-solving techniques vs. more authoritarian and teacher control methods, Jones and Jones (1994) cite Mendler (1992):

> What we must realize is that, while obedience models of discipline always had a down side, in today's world they simply no longer work. The only kids who behave as a result of 'obedience' methods are those who have 'respect' or fear authority. And most of them will stop obeying unless they feel respected by those in authority. Nowadays to be successful in a position of authority requires an ability to connect in a caring way by inspiring hope within others and by leading one's own life in a manner that models the message (xl).

To be successful you must demonstrate that you care

Jones and Jones (1994) go on to discuss reasons why today's students fail to respond to the same authoritarian approaches that worked 20 years ago. Students today are not only more aware of their own rights, but may also associate authoritarian control with physical and psychological abuse and abandonment. In the past, authoritarian homes may still have been stable, loving, and supportive environments. This may not be always true today.
It is not possible within the scope of this literature review to cover all of the approaches currently available for those interested in effectively changing student behaviors. There are many other techniques which offer helpful suggestions for preventing and altering unproductive student behavior, including: behavior management techniques, social skills training, self-management and self-monitoring by students, and school wide student management plans.

The following sources will be helpful for those who want to consider other strategies: Comprehensive Classroom Management: Creating Positive Learning Environments for All Students by Jones & Jones (1995); Solving Discipline Problems by Wolfgang (1995); Looking in Classrooms by Good and Brophy (1994); and Teaching With Love and Logic by Faye & Funk (1995).

Computer-Based Instruction

The use of computers in schools has increased at a tremendous rate. As of the 1992-1993 school year, over 4.4 million computers were installed in the nation's 17,000-plus school districts (SPA, 1993). While computers have been in schools since the Seventies, Means and Olson (1994) indicate the technology of the last two decades has changed the school world far less than it has the worlds of work, entertainment, and communication. Means and Olson explain that early efforts to introduce technology in schools failed for several reasons. First, there was an imperfect match between technological innovations and the bulk of the core curriculum. Software was focused mainly on drill and practice, with an emphasis on very basic skills; consequently, computers were used primarily by students from disadvantaged backgrounds. Also, software which did convey more challenging material such as instructional games, simulations, intelligent tutoring systems, covered only narrow areas and were a poor match with state curriculum guidelines or teacher preferences. Therefore, teachers made few changes in their instructional delivery. Second, reform efforts in the Eighties focused mainly on increasing course requirements in hopes of raising student performance. Educators were not looking to change the basic ways that teaching and learning unfolded.

The Nineties provide a perfect environment for the use of technology. Today's reform efforts strive to change the education system by fostering a different style of teaching (David and Shields, 1991). There is a shift away from classrooms using conventional didactic instructional approaches. The traditional lecture style is being replaced with authentic tasks, multidisciplinary projects, cooperative learning groups, flexible scheduling, and authentic assessments. Technology becomes a valuable tool in such an environment. Peck and Dorricott (1994, p. 12 - 13) give the ten reasons listed below for using technology as an integral part of the learning process.

10
reasons for using technology

1. **"Students learn and develop at different rates."** Technology can individualize instruction through computer networks called integrated learning systems. Computers can track student progress and accumulate records for teachers to use in monitoring progress and planning remedial instruction.

2. **"Graduates must be proficient at accessing, evaluating, and communicating information."** Technology can provoke students to ask in-depth questions, enter into debates, and use higher level problem-solving and critical thinking skills. On-line tools and resources allow students to gather and evaluate information and then effectively communicate their findings through the use of charts, graphs, spreadsheets, and databases.

3. **"Technology can foster an increase in the quantity and quality of students' thinking and writing."** Word processors seem to reduce the phobia often associated with writing. Editing and revising can be done quickly; finished products printed from a word processor look professional and help students feel confident and competent.

4. **"Graduates must solve complex problems."** Technology is one means of helping students develop problem-solving skills. Students can independently organize, analyze, interpret, develop, and evaluate their own work.

5. **"Technology can nurture artistic expression."** Video production, digital photography, and computer-based animation all have great appeal for students and, in addition, provide forms of artistic communication that can increase motivation and foster creative problem-solving.

6. **"Graduates must be globally aware and able to use resources that exist outside the school."** Technology can provide up-to-date maps and demographic data, bring newsroom-quality current events into the classroom, and allow students to learn first-hand about other cultures.

7. **"Technology creates opportunities for students to do meaningful work"**. Students need to produce products that are valued outside of the school environment. Computers can link students to the world, providing them with reasons to write and offering new sources of feedback. As a result, technology lends authenticity to school tasks.

8. **"All students need access to high-level and high-interest courses."** Computers bring novelty and variety to students' school experiences. Laser discs, CD-ROMs, instructional television, distance education technology, animation, and time-lapse photography all bring important learning experiences to students that are not possible with print materials.

9. **"Students must feel comfortable with the tools of the Information Age."** In a world which increasingly relies on computers and other technologies, graduates who are knowledgeableand comfortable with these tools will be far more likely to succeed. As telephone, computer, television and other media begin to merge, the speed, capacity, and reliability of information dissemination will produce incredible new resources. Students taught in the traditional lecture style will be ill-prepared to deal with such a world.

10. **"Schools must increase their productivity and efficiency."** Many of the routine tasks now done by teachers can be reassigned to technology, allowing teachers to spend time on more valuable tasks involving human interaction, continuous evaluation, and improvement of the learning environment.

Several other authors also catalogue the advantages of using computerized instruction. Some additional advantages are:

1. Students can respond more actively and in more varied ways than they can to conventional seat work. Also, computers can provide students with immediate feedback to their responses (Good and Brophy, 1994).

2. Technology makes complex assignments feasible, leading teachers to create assignments involving extensive data collection and analysis. Work can then occur over extended block of time, which is is much more realistic than attempting to fit all projects neatly into a 50 minute time period (Means and Olson, 1994).

3. Technology provides an entry point to content areas and inquiries that might otherwise be inaccessible until later in a student's academic career; consequently, technology can extend and enhance what students are able to produce (Means and Olson, 1994).

More advantages of computerized instruction

Fortunately, there has been extensive research on computer-based instruction, which allows this literature review to use only meta-analysis (the statistical analysis of large collections of results from individual studies) when reviewing both the beneficial and detrimental effects of this particular educational approach. Using the common scale of Effect Size or ES, researchers are able to carry out sophisticated analysis of results from a variety of different studies. ES most often refers to the number of standard deviation units that separates outcome scores of experimental and control groups. The average score of the control group is subtracted from the average score of the experimental group, and the remainder is then divided by the standard deviation of the measure.

What does the research say about computer-based instruction? In the search for answers to this question, only meta-analysis (the statistical analysis of large collections of results from individual studies) were used. In a meta-analysis of 40 comparative studies focusing on the use of computers in elementary schools, Ryan (1991) calculated an average ES of 0.309 for students who received computer based instruction. Bangert-Drowns (1993), in a meta-analysis of the effects of using a word processor as an instructional tool, found an average ES of 0.27 for improvement of writing quality. Bangert-Drowns characterized this effect as small but significant; however, in nine of the studies, the average ES was 0.49.

Computer based instruction has a positive effect on learning

In a summary of at least a dozen separate meta-analysis on the effectiveness of computer-based instruction, Kulik (1994) found that each of the analysis yielded the conclusion that computer-based instruction programs have a positive impact. Kulik lists the major points which emerged from these meta-analysis:

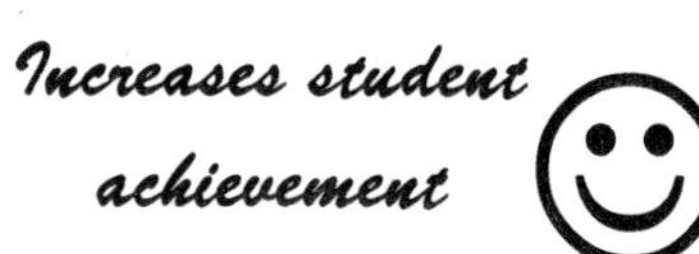

1. **Typically, students learn more in classes offering computer-based instruction.** The low end of the Effect Size was .22, and the high end of the average Effect Size was .57. (An ES of .22 and .57 can be interpreted to mean that the technology-based instruction was 22% and 57% more effective than the control group instruction). The weighted average Effect Size in the 12 meta-analysis was .35. Consequently, the average effect was to raise examination scores by .35 standard deviations, or from the 50th percentile to the 64th (Willett, Yamashita, & Anderson, 1983; Schmidt, Weinstein, Niemiec, and Walberg, 1985).

2. **Students learn their lessons more quickly with computer-based instruction.** In studies of college instruction, the average reduction in instructional time was 34%. In adult education, instruction time was reduced by 24% (C. L. C. Kulik & J. A. Kulik, 1991).

3. **Students like their classes more when they receive computer help.** In 22 studies, the average effects of computer-based instruction was to raise attitude-toward-instruction scores by .28 standard deviations (C. L. C. Kulik & J. A. Kulik, 1991).

4. **When students received help from computers in school, they displayed a more positive attitude towards them.** The average Effect Size in 19 studies on attitude toward computers was .34 (C. L. C. Kulik & J. A. Kulik, 1991).

5. **Computers do not have positive effects in every area in which they were studied** (Kulik & Kulik, 1991).

According to Kulik (1994)

> This review shows that there is a good deal of agreement among meta-analysts on the basic facts about computer-based instruction. All the meta-analysis that I have been able to locate show that adding computer-based instruction to a school program, on the average, improves the results of the program (p. 13).

In an effort to determine which approaches produced better than average results, Kulik (1994) looked more closely at 97 studies carried out in elementary and high schools. Each study was a controlled quantitative study in which outcomes in a class taught with computer-based instruction were compared to outcomes in a class taught without computer-based instruction. Kulik found that in the 97 studies used, computer use could be grouped into six different categories.

1. ***Tutoring*:** The computer presents material, evaluates responses, determines what to present next, and keeps records of progress.

2. ***Managing*:** The computer evaluates students either on-line or off-line, guides students to appropriate instructional resources, and keeps records.

3. ***Simulation*:** The computer generates data that meets student specifications and presents it numerically or graphically in order to illustrate relations in models of social or physical reality.

4. ***Enrichment*:** The computer provides relatively unstructured exercises of various types: games, simulations, and tutoring, etc., to enrich the classroom experience and to stimulate and motivate students.

5. ***Programming*:** Students write short programs in such languages as Basic and Algol to solve mathematics problems. The expectation is that this experience in programming will have positive effects on students' problem-solving abilities and conceptual understanding of mathematics.

6. ***Logo*:** Students give the computer Logo instructions and observe the results on computer screens. From this experience students are expected to gain in ability to solve problems, plan, recognize consequences, and so on... (p.19, 20).

By breaking the studies of computer-based instruction into the six categories, Kulik was able to clarify the evaluation results. He found that **the results for computer tutoring were especially noteworthy**, with the average Effect Size being .38.

Tutoring works

Kulik states that **if a school system is using computers for tutoring, better than average results can be predicted.**

Overall, however, results for the other applications (managing, simulation, programming) were unimpressive. Using computer-managed instruction seldom produced significant positive gains in elementary or high schools. Employing computer simulations in science courses seemed to have little effect on science learning at any level. Programming in Basic or Algol also did not usually produce positive effects on student learning in mathematics courses. Programming in Logo produced only a small effect in most studies, although some did show very high Effect Sizes, probably only because of testing differences. Group tests produced low results, while individually administered tests produced high results.

When comparing computer tutoring with findings on other innovative instructional strategies, Kulik found that few innovations in pre-college teaching have as large of an effect as computer tutorials. Programs of curricular change, such as accelerated classes or classes for gifted students, produced more dramatic effects in evaluation studies, but Kulik warns that these innovations effect only a limited part of the school population. In any case, the effects of computer tutoring were as great as those of peer- and cross-age tutoring and were clearly greater than the gains produced by instructional technologies which rely solely on print materials.

It works!

In an AASA Critical Issues Report, Brodinsky and Keough (1989) suggest that the use of computers is the most effective tool for teaching students at-risk of school failure, often succeeding when all other instructional methods have failed. The advantages of using computers at the center of learning strategies for at-risk students include many of those listed above; however, **the following points regarding computer instruction are particularly relevant for at-risk students:**

6 advantages for using computers with at-risk students

1. Learning is individualized and self-paced.
2. Computer feedback is patient and non-judgmental.
3. The learner is in charge, creating a sense of autonomy important to at-risk students.

4. Computers provide simulations useful in mathematics, science, and social studies, helping to make lessons both interesting and meaningful.
5. Computers enable students to become generators, rather than consumers, of knowledge.
6. The use of word processing tools makes revising and editing written work easy, so students are motivated to write longer and more complex material.

6 advantages for using computers with at-risk students

Kozma and Croninger (1992) also see the benefit of computers for the at-risk student and point out these additional advantages:

1. "The use of interactive multimedia allows students to operate on and see phenomena simultaneously represented in several linked symbol systems (graphs, pictures, sounds). This can help students leverage their current mental structures that are stored in multiple, interconnected, representational forms, thus deepening students understanding" (p. 447).
2. Multimedia has the potential to connect students' school-based learning to "real world" situations. Interactive videos which presents problems embedded in "real world" situations can cue knowledge structures associated with the personal experiences of the student, integrating these with formal, school-based knowledge.
3. Computers provide the opportunity for students to work on tasks which embed the need for basic skills in higher order thinking.
4. Computers offer the possibility for students to work in collaborative groups on goal-oriented tasks. Media can also be used to effectively connect students to family, community, and other cultures.

Multimedia helps students connect to "real world"

Crucial to the success of computer use in schools is the amount of technology training that teachers receive. Ryan (1991) found that teachers with more than 10 hours of computer training significantly outperformed students of teachers with 5 or fewer

Teacher training is crucial

hours of training. In their survey, Cates, McNaull and Gardner (1993) found that, compared to teachers with less training, teachers with more than 3 credit hours of in-service training rated themselves significantly higher on scales of computer expertise and computer comfort. These teachers also had significantly higher opinions of the usefulness of software and reported significantly greater use of computers in the classroom.

Early School Intervention

Note: It is not the purpose of this document to explore interventions that occur prior to the student's entry into school. While such measures may be worthy pursuits, this document examines interventions which can be implemented within the school setting.

Reading failure is preventable

As noted earlier in this document, **school failure can be predicted based on factors observable early in students' school career.** The emphasis in education, however, has been on correction and remediation, rather than on prevention. Considering the research cited by John Pikulski (1994), this is very unfortunate. He states: "This focus on correction rather than prevention continues in spite of an impressive and growing body of authoritative opinion and research evidence which suggests that reading failure is preventable for all but a very small percentage of children (p. 30)" (Clay, 1985; Hall, Prevatte, & Cunningham, 1993; Hiebert, Colt, Catto, & Gurry, 1992; Hiebert & Taylor, 1994; Taylor, Strait, & Medo, 1994; Slavin, Madden, Karweit, Dolan, & Wasik, 1992; Reynolds, 1991; Taylor, Frye, Short, & Shearer, 1992).

Although successful early intervention programs are often expensive, research supports their cost effectiveness when compared with the costs of retention, Chapter I programs, and special education programs (Barnett & Escobar, 1987; Dyer, 1992; Slavin, 1989; Slavin et al., 1992; Smith & Strain, 1988).

Pikulski also looked for evidence of effective remediation programs for students beyond second grade and found very little.

One study by Kennedy, Birman, & Demaline (1986) suggested that remediation efforts beyond third grade are largely unsuccessful.

What types of interventions are most effective?

Testing for School Readiness

Many students' school careers begin with some type of readiness testing that occurs before kindergarten. The use of readiness testing increased dramatically in the Eighties and continues today in many school districts (Gneszda and Bolig, 1988).

When examining the means used to determine readiness for entry to school, two forms of tests are usually employed: developmental screening measures and pre-academic skills tests (Meisels, 1987). Developmental screening measures were originally intended as a first step in evaluating children for potential handicaps, while pre-academic tests were intended for use in planning classroom instruction. Due to the fact that these tests have numerous technical and conceptual problems and that they are being used for purposes for which they were never designed or validated, there are many educators and researchers who are calling for a change in both the substance and purpose of early childhood assessment (Shepard, 1994; Meisels, 1989a; Engel, 1991; Shepard and Graue, 1993). Research scientist Samuel Meisels (1989a) describes such assessment exams as "high-stakes tests" because their results assume greater significance than is warranted and because important and life changing decisions are made for students based on the results.

These tests are being used for purposes which they were not designed or validated!

Shepard (1994) asserts that many of the most popular readiness tests used are actually nothing more than developmental measures taken from old I.Q. tests. Shepard and Graue (1993) compare the popular Gesell School Readiness Screening Test to several intelligence tests and find remarkable similarities. In the Thirties and Forties it was believed that I.Q. tests could accurately measure innate ability, and that this ability was fixed and unalterable. However, as was discussed earlier, recent findings on intelligence demonstrate that intelligence is not innate and immutable, and, more than anything, represents past experience (Gardner, 1983; Sternberg, 1990).

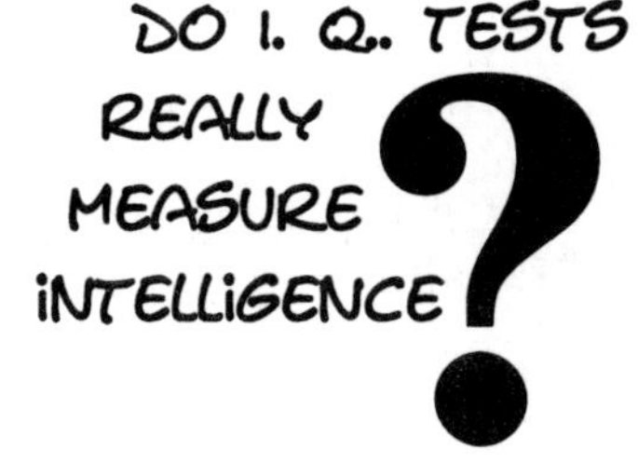

Additionally, the notion of "readiness" for school is also a confusing one. Gesell Institute proponents believe that children who are not ready for school simply need "the gift of time," and that no amount of instruction, intervention, or effort can be expected to have an effect (Meisels, 1989a). However, it has not been proven that readiness is an absolute concept and not a relative one. Readiness is modifiable and, as Shepard (1994) points out, **all of the readiness measures in use are influenced by a child's past learning opportunities.** Unfortunately, this means that a disproportionate number of poor and minority children are either identified as unready and excluded from school when they most need it or are channeled into a two year kindergarten program. As was discussed previously, reviews of these "developmental" programs show no academic benefit for participants (Shepard, 1989b).

Additionally, the Gesell tests have been severely criticized because, despite their wide-spread use, there is a lack of adequate reliability and validity data regarding their effectiveness (Bradley, 1985; Meisels, 1987; Shepard and Smith, 1985; Waters, 1985). Meisels (1989a) also points out that most **readiness tests** are criterion-referenced, where a particular score indicates a specific level of performance mastery. <u>Such tests are meant to measure current achievement, not to predict future performance.</u> He states: **"Therefore, the use of criterion-referenced readiness tests for purposes of classification, retention, and promotion is unjustified."** (18). The <u>Brigance K and 1 Screen</u> is an example of a criterion-referenced test which has been used in such an unintended manner.

Recommendations for Assessing Young Children

According to Shepard (1994), the National Association for the Education of Young Children (the nation's largest professional association of early childhood educators) and the National Association of Early Childhood Specialists in State Departments of Education have played key roles in informing educators about the problems and dangers of a developmentally inappropriate instructional approach and the misuse of tests. In 1991 NAEYC published "Guidelines for Appropriate Curriculum Content and

Assessment in Programs Serving children Ages 3 through 8" (NAEYC, 1991). The guiding principle of this document is that unless there are benefits gained for children (such as the use of information to adjust teaching and learning), then the data should not be collected at all. It states that assessments "should not be used to recommend that children stay out of a program, be retained in grade or be assigned to a segregated group based on ability or developmental maturity" (32).

3 legitimate purposes for assessment

NAEYC acknowledges three legitimate purposes for assessment: **1) to plan instruction and communicate with parents, 2) to identify children with special needs, and 3) to evaluate programs.** The Michigan State Board of Education commissioned an ad hoc Advisory Committee for Early Childhood Standards of Quality to develop Early Childhood Standards of Quality for Pre-kindergarten Through Second Grade (Michigan Department of Education, 1992). This document echoes the message of the NAEYC. Under the "Accountability Standards of Quality," it states that program developers should adhere to the following criterion and indicators:

Criterion B. 1. 1:

Early childhood education programs are expected to be ready for the children; the children are not expected to be ready for the programs.

Does this match what is happening in your school?

Quality Indicators:

Entrance into school is based on chronological age; chidren should not be excluded from school or placed in extra-year programs on the basis of special needs, delayed cognitive, gross, or fine motor skills, home language, or social and emotional development assessment.

Screening procedures, if done at entry, are used to plan appropriate classroom experiences for children or to recommend further evaluation for intervention or special services.

When placements of children are necessary, varied developmentally appropriate methods and techniques for comprehensive screening and diagnostic

> assessment are to be utilized. These procedures are to incorporate the ethnic, cultural, and linguistic differences of the school population.
>
> 
> Decisions for intervention and retention are made by appropriately identifying and assessing the child's functioning level based on the normative developmental range for the child's age group (p. 6).

Samuel Meisels (1989a) believes that before using "high-stakes" tests districts should carefully consider: **1.** the purpose for testing, **2.** the selection of a valid test that is related to the reason for testing, and **3.** the programs options to which children who fail the test will be referred. <u>He recommends that readiness test be seen as a first step in the diagnostic-prescriptive process:</u>

Important

> From this perspective, the purpose of assessing a child's readiness is to understand better what the child does or does not know and can or cannot do, in order to design an instructional program that can increase and enhance the child's knowledge and skills. Using this low stakes model, one assesses readiness to enhance the benefits of instruction, not to prohibit a child from participating in a program. Readiness testing of this kind could result in major positive educational outcomes and could serve accountability needs with criterion-referenced documentation of student progress (p. 20).

There are presently no readiness or achievement tests sufficiently accurate to serve the high-stakes functions they are being asked to perform. Because readiness tests generally do not have predictive validity and are generally used to place children in extra-year programs that do not have demonstrable efficacy, it is Meisels' opinion that the use of such tests for predicting future school performance should be halted. Shepard and Grau (1993) elaborate even further:

> More importantly we stress. . . that validity standards have been broadened in recent years to include more than psychometric accuracy (APA, 1985). If a test is used in a context where it is

> claimed not only that it can distinguish between ready and unready children, but also that ready children should be assigned to treatment A and unready children to treatment B, it must be demonstrated empirically that each group is better off in their respective treatments. If not, then the test cannot be used to make these placement decisions. Given research on program effects, the use of available tests can be defended for the identification of severely and moderately handicapped children. **But there is not evidence to support the use of tests to delay school entry, to place children in readiness rooms or transition grades, to retain children in kindergarten, or to assign children to segregated at-risk classrooms** (p. 304).

IT DOES NOT WORK!

Meisels (1989a) does believe, however, that there are reliable and valid developmental screening tests which, when administered by trained testers to individual children before entry to school, can identify children who are at high risk for school failure (1988, 1989b). His recommendation is to then move on to a more comprehensive diagnostic process in order to determine the exact nature of their problems and, subsequently, to obtain the appropriate interventions.

Effective Early School Prevention Programs

Once a child formally begins his or her school career, what does the research say about effective interventions at early levels? Pikulski (1994) compared five school-based early intervention programs, each of which presented data suggesting that they were "effective" or led to substantially better reading achievement than those of similar students who had not participated in the program. Pikulski presents the common features identified from all five programs rather than trying to prove which program is best. He recommends that school districts choose programs based on district circumstances, selecting the program which best fits their individual needs.

It is Pikulski's opinion that attention to the following issues will increase the probability of program success:

Coordinated Instruction

1. **Consider the total reading instruction program when planning for early intervention.** Maximum impact is gained when early intervention programs try to ensure that students receive excellent and coordinated instruction both in their classrooms and in the special intervention programs.

Some need extra time

2. **Provide more reading instruction time for children having reading difficulties than children who are not experiencing difficulty.** In this extra time it is important that they receive quality instruction.

Small groups

3. **It is essential to provide individual or very small group (no more than 4 or 5 students) instruction for at-risk children**. Some children will need one-to-one tutoring.

First grade most important

4. **Focus special reading instruction for at-risk students while in first grade**. Where school resources are limited, the priority should be on first-grade interventions which lead to the prevention of reading difficulties. (Some students will need support beyond first grade.)

They must experience success

5. **Select simple texts for early intervention programs**. Predictable texts are most effective in the beginning stages. Interesting literature with natural language patterns seems important, and texts constructed to encourage application of word identification skills may also be beneficial.

Develops fluency

6. **At-risk children should read the same text several times to develop reading fluency**. It is important to use instructional procedures which ensure that students see reading as an act of constructing meaning.

Word Attack Skills

7. **Reading instruction for at-risk students should focus attention on words and letters**. Phonemic awareness and phonics instruction, as well as focusing on word patterns, all appear to have merit.

8. **Writing should be emphasized in early intervention programs**. Writing words helps children to attend to the details of those words, thus supporting the development of word identification skills. Student writing should occur daily; these activities should be brief, and the instruction should focus student attention on features and details of letters and words.

Writing important

9. **Monitor student progress through ongoing assessment.** The assessment of oral reading fluency is informative and effective.

Assessment

10. **Communication between home and school is essential**. Materials for daily reading at home should be provided to students.

Communicate with parents

11. **Staff early intervention programs with professionally prepared and accomplished teachers.** Initial training and continuing professional support should be provided so that teachers learn to deliver consistently effective instruction.

Continuous staff development

Emergent Literacy and Developmentally Appropriate Kindergarten

There has been much research on the effectiveness of programs and practices designed for kindergartners. This is especially important since current research does not support practices such as placing students in a two-year kindergarten or retaining them. The first of our national goals for education states that by the year 2000 all children will start school ready to learn.

Changes that schools need to make

In a report done by the Southern Regional Education Board in Atlanta, Georgia (1994), it is emphasized that schools must also be ready to meet the needs of all children, including those who are not deemed ready. The report goes on to cite changes that schools need to make in their kindergarten programs in order to achieve our national goal. The first change recommended is that all schools should implement developmentally appropriate curriculum, instruction, and assessment practices at the kindergarten through third grade levels. <u>Our kindergartens need to be</u>

prepared for all students, not just those capable of handling kindergarten which have become too academically challenging over the years for some entering students.

Significant changes in early childhood and reading education

How our kindergarten approaches are helping students to read should be a primary focus when looking at developmentally appropriate kindergarten. Recently, there has been a significant revolution in the fields of early childhood and reading education (Spodek and Saracho, 1993). These changes greatly influence and effect our early childhood philosophies and practices.

The past decade has seen a shift in how we view the literacy development of young children. We have moved from a "reading readiness" perspective to an "emergent literacy" one. Research in emergent literacy (see Mason & Allen, 1986; Strickland & Morrow, 1989; Sulzby, 1991) has changed the way educators look at literacy development in children. **Skills are not seen as prerequisites to reading, but as a part of developing literacy.** Young children are treated as readers and writers long before they can read from a book on their own. Research on brain-based learning supports many of the new ideas on literacy developments. New findings about how the brain works have many implications for how kindergarten classrooms are managed. Teale and Sulzby (1989) outline the distinctive dimensions of this new research on early literacy:

1. The age range studied now includes children younger than 14 months.
2. Literacy is no longer regarded as simply a cognitive skill, but as a complex activity with social, linguistic, and psychological aspects.
3. Literacy learning is perceived as multidimensional and tied to the child's natural surroundings, so it is studied in both the home and school environments.

Consequently, children can be introduced to print material at a very early age, contrary to early beliefs that this would be harmful. **However, literacy related materials in kindergarten classrooms should not look like the worksheets or workbook pages that were found in so many classrooms a few years ago.**

Strickland (1990) summarizes the new insights into how young children learn to read and write with this new perspective:

1. **Learning how to read and write begins early in life and continues as an on-going process.** Living in a "print-rich" environment causes literacy learning to occur as a natural part of children's daily lives.

2. **Reading and writing are interrelated processes which develop simultaneously with oral language**. The language processes of listening, speaking, reading and writing develop in an interdependent manner; each informing and supporting the other. This contrasts with the conventional view that one must precede the other for effective learning to occur. The child does not have to be orally fluent before being introduced to reading and writing.

Listening, speaking, reading and writing develop in an interdependent manner.

3. **Active participation in meaningful early life activities is essential to learning how to read and write**. Using reading and writing to construct meaning in the child's life makes the activity more significant and, as a result, more effective.

4. **Interaction with responsive others is important in learning to read and write**. Parents, care-givers and teachers need to interact meaningfully with the young child's early attempts at reading and writing (e.g. "reading" books by picture reading or scribbling messages).

MEANINGFUL INTERACTION ESSENTIAL

5. **Shared book experiences can greatly enhance learning to read and write**.

Snow and Tabors (1993) write about the relation of language development to literacy development. They argue that the emergence of the various domains of language into conscious awareness is one of the important achievements of early childhood years. They believe that this "metalinguistic awareness" is one major conduit between oral language and literacy. When children become aware of words in an abstract way, they have developed metaphonological awareness, which is demonstrated by things such as practicing rhyming words or listing words beginning with the same sound. Snow and Tabor state:

Understanding sound/symbol correspondence is essential

> Such meta-phonological awareness is a direct route into the sound-symbol correspondences crucial to reading. And there is a great deal of evidence that the ability to raise to consciousness information about the abstract phonemic structure of words relates to ease of reading acquisition (Blachman, 1984; Bradley & Bryant, 1983; Vellutino & Scanlon, 1987, p.8).

Early predictor of reading ability

There is also evidence that phonological awareness in kindergarten predicts reading ability later (Blachman, 1983; Bradley & Bryant, 1985; Mann, 1991). Children can also discover these sound-symbol correspondences by attempting to write.

The emergent literacy perspective helps us to see that assisting children develop a wide variety of oral language abilities is a crucial precursor to literacy development. It is also important to make children aware of these connections. There are many ways to do this in an early childhood classroom. Morrow and Rand (1993) offer the following suggestions for preparing teachers to support the literacy development of young children:

4 things teachers can do to support literacy development of young children.

1. **Daily story reading and storytelling** with felt boards, puppets, and props can attract young children to books and provide active involvement for different learning styles (Morrow, 1989). Becoming a competent reader requires active involvement, practice, and motivation (Anderson, Hiebert, Scott, & Wilkinson, 1985).

2. **Independent time for reading and writing** should be provided, during which children can choose the literacy activities in which they want to participate, such as looking at books, listening to taped stories, or dramatizing stories. These types of activities promote achievement in reading (Morrow, 1992).

3. **Children need plenty of time to become actively involved in the development of writing skills**. At the earliest stages, this could simply be a child scribbling and

then relating its meaning. In emergent literacy theory, reading and writing are linked. As children experiment with writing, they refine their knowledge of written language, which, in turn, helps to make reading possible. Writing centers, stocked with paper, writing tools, and envelopes encourage children to explore and play with writing.

4. **Social interactions in real-life and meaningful experiences are critical in learning to read** (Smith, 1983). Holdaway (1979) identified four processes related to social interaction that facilitate the acquisition of literacy:

   a. Children need to observe adults or peers involved in their own literacy activities.

   b. They need to collaborate with others in a socially inter active manner.

   c. They need to practice literacy behaviors alone or with other.

   d. They need to share literacy through performances, such as by reading what they have written to a friend. Social collaboration can be encouraged in the classroom by reading stories one-on-one or in small-groups, and by encouraging responses, participation and elaboration. Also, dramatic play themes could be supported by print-related props (e.g. menus, note pads, etc.).

We must provide a print rich environment for at-risk students

According to Snow & Perlmann (1985), early readers tend to come from homes where language is stimulated, encouraged, and used as a component of everyday living to accomplish tasks and communicate in a meaningful way. At-risk students may come from environments where this type of stimulation is lacking. Therefore, it makes it even more imperative that we provide a "print-rich" environment with literacy learning integrated into everything that occurs throughout the day.

Karweit (1989) emphasizes that kindergarten is critical for students who may encounter later academic difficulties because it provides the basis for success in the elementary curriculum which follows. In general, Karweit states that effective kindergarten practices incorporate specific materials, management plans, activities, and structures. These programs are not rigid, but they are still specific. **Lower socio-economic students were found to benefit in particular from a structured curricular approach, meaning programs which are both detailed and specific.**

Continuous Progress

Continuous progress, or non-graded schooling, attracted interest throughout the Sixties and Seventies, and has recently started to receive serious attention again. Typically used in primary grades, a non-graded school does not use grade level designations for students or classes. Students are flexibly grouped according to performance rather than age and proceed with less stigmatization at their own rate. Individual differences are typically accommodated by adjusting an integrated and thematic curriculum, and students must reach a certain level of academic performance before entering fourth grade.

Longitudinal studies show consistent positive achievement effects when using the Continuous Progress method when compared to traditional grouping, including lower anxiety and higher self-esteem (Pavan, 1992).

In their meta-analysis, Gutierrez and Slavin (1993) determined that the nongraded program was a significant factor in student success, with the strongest and most consistent positive effects occurring when the program focused on grouping children according to performance in one or more subjects, rather than on providing individualized instruction. Educational Research Newsletter, in reviewing Gutierrez and Slavin, stated:

> . . . the achievement differences between nongraded programs are due to the amount of direct teacher instruction children receive as opposed to the amount of time spent working independently on seat work. Grouping across age and grade lines apparently allows teachers to reduce the number of within class groups they teach at any given time. This in turn reduces the amount of time students spend on seat work and increases the amount of direct teacher contact. Cross age groupings can

> totally eliminate within-class grouping, enabling teachers to spend the entire reading period working with the whole class on developmentally appropriate activities p. (2).

While students in such programs tend to complete the primary grades in the normal time, those who might normally fall behind in traditional settings can receive extra help without stigma. An effective nongraded program demonstrates not only an effective organization, but also a developmentally appropriate curriculum and instructional methods which provide appropriate and rich educational experiences.

Effective Chapter I Programs

(Chapter I has recently been renamed Title I. Since it is still referred to in the literature as Chapter I, this document it will continue to use Chapter I.)

Several consistent themes emerge when one looks at the research-based knowledge about programs that work in compensatory education settings. In 1985 the U.S. Department of Education identified exemplary Chapter I program sites, the results of which are reviewed by Crawford (1989). The study resulted in the identification of characteristics of effective compensatory education programs. Stringfield and Yoder (1992) describe additional studies (Hepler et al., 1987; Stringfield, Yoder, & Quilling, 1989; Stringfield et al., 1989) which looked for evidence of the same characteristics as well as any additional components that contributed to the programs' successes. These consistent themes, combined from the above studies, are as follows.

What Works

Organizational/Leadership Level

All children can and will learn

1. **The primary goal of the Chapter I program leader** (which could be the principal or program director) **was that each student could and would learn.** This mes-

sage was consistently sent to teachers of Chapter I programs. Objectives followed from this goal as well as resources to accomplish it.

Strong instructional leaders

2. Principals or directors were exceptionally good instructional leaders. They were knowledgeable and active in ongoing efforts to find the most potentially useful instructional options.

Highly qualified teachers

3. Leaders made sure that programs were staffed with highly qualified and experienced teachers who were supported and encouraged in providing quality instruction.

Staff development critical

4. Staff development was an integral component, with assessment of teacher needs and effective training strategies employed. Regularly scheduled training sessions and faculty meetings were common in effective Chapter I programs. Planning time for teachers was also provided.

Accountability

5. Leaders held teachers accountable for students' learning.

Coordination

6. The education of at risk students was seen as everyone's responsibility, Consequently, consistent and formal coordination between Chapter I and classroom teachers was required.

Monitor and adjust

7. Programs were consistently monitored for successful instruction. Classroom visits and careful study of student progress led to program adjustment. Successful practices were maintained and formalized.

Discard what is not working

8. Methods, materials, and staff that were not effective in meeting the needs of the students were replaced with more promising options.

Parent involvement

9. Intelligent parent involvement was encouraged by program leaders through newsletters, positive notes, and letters to parents explaining how to help teach their child.

Instructional/Classroom Practices

1. The primary purpose of instruction was to develop individual student's academic skills. Teachers were encouraged to identify individual students strengths and weaknesses, and to try a variety of resources and techniques if students were unsuccessful. Some of the approaches mentioned included interactive teaching (a combination of direct instruction and active teaching), flexible grouping, individualized instruction, mastery learning, cross-age tutoring and computer assisted instruction for individual pacing and increased student motivation. Significant efforts were made by teachers on students' behalf and support was provided to teachers when needed.

   Adjust instructional strategies to meet student needs

2. Planning for students' educational goals specifically included diagnosis, prescriptive planning, delivery of instruction and evaluation of student progress in a continuing and interconnected process.

   Diagnosis and prescriptive teaching

3. Lesson design included success, challenge, and high expectations of students.

   Challenge & success

4. The use of praise and rewards associated with student goal accomplishments was evident, however, it was used judiciously and only when it was truly called for.

   Praise & rewards

5. The coordination between the Chapter I teachers and the regular classroom teachers was frequent and intensive.

   Coordination

6. Local programs often used nationally recognized instructional programs, however, the programs were used when and where they were judged to be needed.

   Nationally recognized

7. Teachers made maximum use of academic learning time by thoughtful scheduling, assessing student success, teaching on task behaviors, and eliciting parents to monitor homework.

   Time on task

In a review of the existing literature, Archambault (1989) tried to determine what is known about the effectiveness of certain features of compensatory education programs. He cautioned that the translation of research into practice is a risky business, especially when evidence in not clear-cut; however, he also acknowledged that educators want and are in need of help, and that they cannot always wait for unambiguous research results. With this in mind, he cautiously offered the following advice:

Effective practices are of prime importance

1. **Setting**: Many districts are moving towards push-in programs as opposed to pull-out programs in an effort to counteract the negative effects associated with removing students from their classroom (See page 30 on traditional Chapter I Pullout programs). However, based on his research findings, Archambault concludes that setting is not directly responsible for student outcomes — the issue of effective practices within settings, and not the settings themselves, are of prime importance.

2. **Specialists and Aides**: There is little evidence detailing what combination of instructors and conditions are likely to maximize student performance. The key issue is to determine which option is likely to deliver the highest quality instruction to the student, and this may vary from district to district. Archambault found that the issues which are particularly germane to these decisions are: **"which program will ensure the greatest amount of engaged time in specific subject areas; the best communication, cooperation, and coordination among the regular and compensatory program; the greatest integration of instruction across these two domains; and the fewest negative consequences such as the stigma attached to receiving compensatory instruction.** (p. 255)."

3. **Class Size and Grouping**: Educationally disadvantaged students benefit from classes that contain less than fifteen students and are heterogeneous in ability. Classes of five students or less, which is the typical class size for Chapter I groups, produce the most dramatic effects, although within-class ability grouping for reading and math and cross-grade grouping is also beneficial.

4. **Individualization**: Individualization is effective in classrooms with small student/teacher ratios because close supervision is possible. It is not effective when the

burden of progress is placed on the student, who is forced to spend extended periods of time on worksheets and other published materials. **The teacher must play an active role in instruction and not allow the materials to do the teaching.**

Summary

It is difficult to know what specific characteristics at-risk students will exhibit. These characteristics are complex and will vary from building to building, and even from year to year. Consequently, it is necessary to gather information and continuously monitor specific risk factors among a district's students. Certain critical factors have been shown to have greater predictive power than others, including poverty, academic performance, attendance, self-concept, motivation, anti-social behavior, school disengagement, home educational environment, family make-up, frequent moves along with scheduled transitions, and latch-key situations.

Risk factors

The research tells us that it is especially important to look at students who demonstrate multiple risk factors because they face a far greater likelihood of school failure. When such student data is collected and correlated with school achievement — as shown by grades, test scores, and reading levels — we can recognize our at-risk students and understand their needs. The needs of at-risk students will vary from school to school and from year to year, creating the need for continued longitudinal studies. Better data will lead to better distribution of district resources.

Data analysis

Research tells us, without a doubt, that all children can learn. It logically follows then that we must take each student who comes to us, adapt the school environment to them for a "best fit," and use what we know from research to help determine which intervention would be most appropriate for that student. The school must adapt to and be more tolerant of individual student differences in learning rates and styles, multiple intelligences, and cultural heritage. The Ecological model allows us to look broadly at the interactive environments that affect the student, including the classroom, building, district, and community.

Adapt to needs of students

To ensure a "fit" between the district's model, students' at-risk profiles, and possible interventions, it is necessary for a district to ask the following questions, suggested by Sagor (1993):

1. Is the proposed strategy consistent with our theory of at-riskness?
2. Is there empirical evidence to support our belief that it will work in this setting?

Research demonstrates that certain interventions can be discarded as ineffective. In fact, it has been shown conclusively that many commonly used practices either do not work and may even be detrimental. If we decide to use any of these discredited interventions, we owe it to our students to demonstrate with hard data that they do, in fact, work in that particular setting.

Some of these discredited practices include: retention, full day kindergarten programs, two-year kindergarten tracks, Chapter I pull-out programs, and special education for mildly learning disabled students

Questionable practices

We also need to look seriously at interventions which may have harmful effects, including: inflexible curriculums, bell curve grading, ability grouping and tracking, and discipline policies that lead to disengagement.

Although interventions must be targeted to the specific needs of a district's at-risk population, research does offer guidelines for the essential factors present in the most successful programs. Successful programs:

Essential factors for successful programs

1. are comprehensive,
2. begin early,
3. have high expectations,
4. emphasize continuous progress rather than remediation,
5. encourage home/school partnerships,
6. focus on motivation and student responsibility for learning,
7. Emphasize positive self-concept and school climate,

8. attempt to fulfill student's basic psychological needs, especially social bonding,
9. empower teachers and principals to be active decision makers,
10. are aggressively led,
11. use data analysis to demonstrate student growth socially, behaviorally and academically.

As district responses to the at-risk population are developed, we should not only have a clear focus on district beliefs and philosophies, but also on the essential factors of successful at-risk programs. Along with the use of hard data to back up our decisions and direction, these guidelines will allow us to keep moving in the right direction.

The following is a summary of interventions designed to increase student achievement.

It Works!

Mastery Learning is a well-documented approach in which high performance becomes the norm. The four critical variables which must be present in this program are:

1. **Motivation** - helping students see value and purpose in mastering the curriculum.
2. **Prerequisite Skills** - ensuring that students are not missing the critical skills needed to master material.
3. **Quality instruction** - providing instruction that is appropri ate to the learner's culture, cognitive level, learning style, etc.
4. **Adequate time** - believing that, given adequate time, anyone can learn a skill or acquire knowledge.

These all seem especially relevant to the at-risk learner. **The literature tells us that at-risk students do better when they see the value of what they are doing; that they often enter school lacking critical skills; that we need to be cognizant of their individual differences; and that finally, and perhaps most importantly, students can learn if given adequate time.**

Keeping in mind new findings which show that intelligence is not fixed and that, when it is measured, it often reflects lack of past experiences and poverty levels more than ability, the above critical variables become very significant indeed. The variable which most often remains lacking, however, is providing students with enough time to master core outcomes. As Blokker says in his at-risk seminars: "We need to make time the variable and learning the constant, rather than the reverse."

Promising intervention

Outcome-Based Education is a macro-level process involving overall planning and restructuring of school or district policy. Mastery Learning is a vital component of OBE. First, crucial exit outcomes are determined, then the curriculum is organized around those outcomes. There are three versions of OBE which range from completely restructuring the entire school, to simply allowing the existing curriculum to dictate the planning process. These variations, along with a complex student assessment environment, make evaluating OBE difficult for researchers. Nonetheless, the model holds great promise for maximizing learning for all students.

Promising intervention

Authentic Assessment requires students to demonstrate specific skills or competencies in an open-ended situation. This type of assessment tends to resemble real learning tasks, requires complex and challenging mental processes, acknowledges more than one approach, and places more emphasis on real products. Intense interest in Authentic Assessment has arisen due to advances in cognitive science and the belief that improved assessment will call forth higher quality instruction. Researchers are in agreement about Authentic Assessment's definite promise and its potential benefits for at-risk learners.

Appears to have merit

Multicultural Education aims to help students from diverse backgrounds attain equal educational opportunities and to help all students develop positive cross cultural attitudes and behaviors. One of the most important needs for at-risk students is to develop a sense of belonging. Multicultural Education creates an atmosphere where all students not only feel that they belong, but also that everyone belongs, regardless of their race or ethnicity.

The Multicultural Education movement is too new to have research support at this time; however, it appears to have merit not only for the at-risk students, but for all other students as well.

Learning Style theorists believe that all individuals have a preference to learn in a particular way, including visually, orally, spatially, and tactiley. Because at-risk students' learning styles seem to be the ones most mismatched with predominant teaching styles, there are those who believe they have the most to gain from the application of Learning Style Theory. Approaches to classroom implementation range from recommendations to match student learning styles with teacher instruction, to assisting students in becoming capable of benefiting from all learning styles. Unfortunately, there is little agreement among Learning Style Theory models, and testing instruments not only lack validity and reliability, but also measure different characteristics depending on what test is given. Consequently, there is little solid empirical evidence to support Learning Style Theory.

We need more info on this . . the jury is still out!

Cooperative Learning involves students working in groups or teams to achieve specific educational goals and to develop positive interdependence as they learn to rely on each another. With Cooperative Learning, the typical classroom teaching and learning activities are supplemented in such a way that much of the individual seat work is replaced. The empirical evidence supporting Cooperative Learning is staggering at all grade levels, in all major subject areas, and in key affective domains. Two vital elements to successful cooperative programs are group goals and individual accountability — in other words, groups are rewarded based on the individual learning of all group members. **However, unless sufficient attention is paid to individual and group accountability, Cooperative Learning will actually be detrimental to at-risk students.**

It Works!

Community Service Learning enables students to discover that they are useful, contributing members of a social community. Community service programs are especially powerful for at-risk students and often include many successful drop out prevention practices. By becoming service providers, at-risk children can see themselves as protagonists who can take an active

Promising intervention

role in making things better for themselves as well as others. Research findings indicate that student service is a viable strategy that not only contributes to academic learning, but also to character development. However, flaws do exist in this model due to methodological problems.

teachers can motivate students . . . but need staff development to learn how

Student Motivation Strategies attempt to boost the degree to which students invest attention and effort in school. ***A teacher's skill in motivating students to learn is key to the the teacher's effectiveness.*** Students must expect to be able to perform successfully if they apply themselves and must value either the task itself or the rewards that come from successful completion. Four preconditions necessary for successful use of motivational strategies are: supportive environments, appropriate levels of challenge or difficulty, meaningful learning objectives, and moderation and variation in strategy use. There are a variety of strategies which teachers can employ in order to help students develop a link between their effort and outcome. Among them are:

1. Teacher modeling and feedback,
2. Portraying effort as an investment rather than as a risk,
3. Portraying skill development as incremental,
4. Focusing on mastery, and
5. Attributional retraining. This includes concentrating on task, coping with failure, attributing failures to insufficient effort and successes to personal effort.

Promote intrinsic motivation

Goal setting and commitment have been shown to play an important role in developing self-motivation and increasing performance. Ultimately, we want students to develop intrinsic motivation; however, since at-risk students often do not value school experiences, extrinsic motivation may be the simplest method to encourage task engagement. Teachers should be aware of the guidelines for appropriate use of extrinsic rewards and also methods to develop intrinsic motivation. Many common classroom practices promote intrinsic motivation, such as active participation, emphasis on higher-level objectives, frequent feedback, use of game-like practice activities, use of project-based learning, simulation, and peer interaction opportunities.

<u>**Discipline and Conflict**</u> are important factors in a student's decision to leave school. Discipline policies can increase the likelihood that at-risk students with behavioral problems will continue in a downward spiral. At-risk students are often disengaged from and at odds with school norms and rules. Educators need to evaluate their district's discipline plans to determine if these policies actually serve to increase incidences of disengagement.

We must evaluate our policies and procedures

Computer-Based Instruction can be a valuable tool for raising student performance. When students receive computer-based instruction, they not only learn more in less time, but also like classes better. Computer-based tutoring has been shown to significantly improve learning gains. There are many reasons to employ technology as an integral component of the learning process for all students, especially for students classified as at-risk. Some of these reasons include:

It Works!

1. Learning is individualized and self-paced.
2. Computer feedback is patient and non-judgmental.
3. Learners develop a sense of autonomy.
4. Simulations make lessons interesting and meaningful.
5. Students become generators of knowledge.
6. Revising and editing written work is easier.
7. Development of problem-solving and higher order thining skills is enhanced.
8. Artistic expression is nurtured.

<u>**Early School Prevention**</u> focuses efforts at the K-3 level to prevent school failure. Since <u>reading failure is preventable</u> for all but a very small percentage of children and remediation programs for students beyond second grade are largely unsuccessful, expensive early intervention programs are very cost-effective.

Reading failure is preventable

While testing for school readiness in order to determine if a child can enter school is common in many districts, research simply does not support the use of readiness tests for this purpose; instead, they should be used solely to plan suitable classroom experiences or to recommend further evaluation for possible intervention or special services. Both state and national early childhood specialists agree that entrance into school should be based solely upon chronological age, and children should not be excluded from school or placed in extra year programs on the basis of special needs, home background, or developmental delays.

Features of effective early intervention programs

Effective early level interventions have been found to share these common features:

1. High quality, coordinated reading instruction.
2. Extra reading instruction time allocated for those experencing difficulty.
3. Individual or very small group instructional for at-risk children.
4. Special reading instruction focused on first grade, where it is the most profitable.
5. Early intervention texts that are easy to read.
6. Multiple reading of the same texts to obtain the greatest benefits.
7. Instruction for at-risk students should focus on phonemic awareness, phonics and word patterns.
8. Ample opportunities for writing.
9. Ongoing assessment which continually monitors student progress.
10. Excellent communication between the home and the school.
11. Good teachers.

Developmentally appropriate kindergarten, with an emphasis on an **Emergent Literacy** approach to reading and writing, are essential for meeting the needs of all children.

These work!

Continuous Progress or **Non-Graded Schools** have also shown consistently positive achievement effects, especially when the focus is on grouping children according to performance rather than on providing individualized instruction. As noted earlier, Continuous Progress Schools provide one manner of making <u>time</u> the variable and <u>learning</u> the constant.

This review of existing at-risk literature is intended to be comprehensive. Nonetheless, its greatest value will be to serve as a starting point for serious discussion within the district on the priorities and directions needed for better meeting the needs of <u>all</u> students. If we are to make good on our commitment to educate our community's children, we must act upon the assumption that all children can learn, regardless of their individual characteristics or backgrounds.

By adopting a systemic approach to change that is rooted in practices supported by existing research, we should be able to significantly raise academic achievement levels for each and every student — whether they are at-risk or not — throughout our entire school system.

References

Agnew, E. M. (1981). The Relationship Between Elementary School Climate and School Achievement. (Doctoral dissertation, University of San Francisco). Dissertation Abstracts International, 43, 360A.

Aksamit, D. (1990). "Mildly Handicapped and At-Risk Students: The Graying of the Line," Academic Therapy, 25, 277-289.

Alderman, M. K. (1990). "Motivation for At-Risk Students," Educational Leadership, 48 (1), 27-30.

Aleem, D., & Moles, O. (1993). Review of Research on Ways to Attain Goal Six: Creating Safe, Disciplined, and Drug-Free Schools. Washington, DC: OERI.

Alexander, L., Frankiewicz, R., & Williams, R. (1979). "Facilitation of Learning and Retention of Oral Instruction Using Advance and Post Organizers," Journal of Educational Psychology, 71, 701-707.

Amabile, T. M. (1985). "Motivation and Creativity: Effects of Motivational Orientation on Creative Writers." Journal of Personality and Social Psychology. 48: 393-399.

American Psychological Association, American Research Association, & National Council on Measurement in Education. (1985). Standards for Educational and Psychological Testing. Washington, DC: American Psychological Association.

Ames, C. (1984). "Competitive, Cooperative, and Individualistic Goal Structures: A Cognitive-Motivational Analysis," in R. Ames & C. Ames (Eds.), Research on Motivation in Education. Vol. 1: Student Motivation. New York: Academic Press.

Ames, C. and Ames, R. (Eds). (1989). Research on Motivation in Education. Vol. 3 Goals and Cognitions. San Diego: Academic Press.

Anderson, C. S. (1982). "The Search for School Climate: A Review of the Research," Review of Educational Research. 52 (3), 368-420. Anderson, S. (1985). "The Investigation of School Climate," In Gilbert R. Austin and Herbert Garber (Eds.), Research on Exemplary Schools. New York: Academic Press.

Anderson, R. C., Hiebert, E. H., Scott, J. A., & Wilkinson, I. (1985). Becoming a Nation of Readers. Washington, DC: National Institute of Education.

Apple, M. (1990). Ideology and Curriculum. 2nd ed. New York: Routledge.

Applebee, A. M.; Langor, J. A. and Mullis, I. V. S. (1988). Who Reads Best? Factors Related to Reading Achievement in Grades 3, 7, and 11. Princeton, NJ:Educational Testing Service.

Apter, S. J. (1982). Troubled Children/Troubled Systems. New York: Pergamon.

Archambault, F. X. Jr. (1989). "Instructional Setting and Other Design Features of Compensatory Education Programs," In Slavin, R. E., Karweit, N. L. and Madden, N. A. (Eds.) Effective Programs for Students at Risk. Boston: Allyn and Bacon.

Archbald, D.A. and Newmann, F. M. (1988). Beyond Standardized tests. Reston, VA: National Association of Secondary School Principals.

Association for Supervision and Curriculum Development. (1993). ASCD 1993 Resolutions. Alexandria. VA: Author.

Ausubel, D., Novak, J., & Hanesian, G. (1978). Educational Psychology: A Cognitive View. New York: Holt, Rinehart and Winston.

Ayala-Canales, C. E. (1984). The Impact of El Salvador's Civil War on Orphan and Refugee Children. M. S. Thesis in Child Development, University of California at Davis.

Baas, A. (1991). "Promising Strategies For At-Risk Youth," ERIC Digest. No. 59.

Bachman, J. G.; Green, S.; and Wertanen, I. D. (1971). Youth in Transition, Dropping Out-Problem or Symptom? Vol. 3 Ann Arbor, Michigan: Institute for Social Research.

Bachman, J. G.; Green, Swayzer; and Wirtanen, I. D. (1971). Dropping Out-Problem or Symptom? Youth in Transition Vol. 3. Ann Arbor, Mi.: Institute for Social Research , University of Michigan.

Baer, J. (1988). "Let's Not Handicap Able Thinkers," Educational Leadership, 45 (7), 66-72.

Banathy, B. H. (1991). Systems Design of Education: A Journey to Create the Future. Englewood Cliffs, NJ: Educational Technology Publications.

Bandura, A. (1986). Social Foundations of Thought and Action. Englewood Cliffs, NJ: Prentice Hall.

Bandura, A. (1989). "Human Agency in Social Cognitive Theory," American Psychologist, 44, 1175-1184.

Bandura, A. and Schunk, D. (1981). "Cultivating Competence, Self-Efficacy, and Intrinsic Interest Through Proximal Self-Motivation," Journal of Personality and Social Psychology, 41, 586-598.

Bangart-Drowns, R. L. (1993). "The Word Processor as an Instructional Tool: A Meta-Analysis of Word Processing in Writing Instruction," Review of Educational Research. 63 (1). 69-93.

Banks, J. A. (1991). "Multicultural Education: Its Effects on Students' Racial and Gender Role Attitudes". In Handbook of Research on Social Teaching and Learning, edited by J. P. Shaver. New York: Macmillan.

Banks, J. A. (1993). "Multicultural Education: Development, Dimensions, and Challenges. Phi Delta Kappan. September, 1993, pp. 22-28.

Banks, J. A. (1994). "Transforming the Mainstream Curriculum," Educational Leadership 51, 8: 4-8.

Banks, J. A. and Banks, C. A. M. (Eds). (1989). Multicultural Education: Issue and Perspectives. Boston: Allyn & Bacon.

Barnett, W. S. and Escobar, C. M. (1987). "The Economics of Early Educational Intervention: A Review of Educational Research 57: 387-414.

Barr, R. and Dreeben, R. (1983). How Schools Work. Chicago, IL: University of Chicago Press.

Barro, S. and Kolstad, A. (1987). Who Drops Out of High School? Findings from High School and Beyond (Report No. CS 87-397c). Washington, D. C. : US

Bates, J. A. (1979). "Extrinsic Reward and Intrinsic Motivation: A Review with Implications for the Classroom." Review of Educational Research 19: 557-576.

Bauer, D. H. (1976). "An Exploratory Study of Developmental Changes in Children's Fears," Journal of Child Psychology and Psychiatry, 17, 69-74.

Becker, H. J. (1987). Addressing the Needs of Different Groups of Early Adolescents: Effects of Varying School and Classroom Organizational Practices on Students from Different Social Background and Abilities (Report No. 16). Baltimore, Md.: Center for Research on Elementary and Middle Schools, Johns Hopkins University.

Becker, W., Engelman, S. & Thomas, D. (1975). Teaching 1: Classroom Management. Champaign, IL: Research Press.

Benard, B. (1991). Fostering Resiliency in Kids: Protective Factors in the Family, School, and Community. Position Paper for Western Center for Drug-Free Schools and Communities. Washington, DC: Department of Education.

Benard, B. (1993). "Fostering Resiliency in Kids," Educational Leadership, Vol. 51, (3), pp. 44-48.

Bensen, G. P., Hawcraft, J. R., Steyaert, J. P., & Weigel, D. J. (1979). "Mobility in Sixth Graders as Related to Achievement, Adjustment, and Socioeconomic Status," Psychology in the Schools, 16, 444-447.

Bergen, D. (1994). "Authentic Performance Assessments," Childhood Education. Winter, 93/94, pp.99-102.

Berk, F. A., ed. (1986). Performance Assessment: Methods and Applications. Baltimore, Md.: The John Hopkins University Press.

Bettencourt, E., Gillett, M., Gall, M.,& Hull, R. (1983). "Effects of Teacher Enthusiasm Training on Student On-Task Behavior and Achievement," American Educational Research Journal, 20, 435-450.

Betts, E. (1946). Foundations of Reading Instruction. New York: American Book.

Betts, F. (1992). "How Systems Thinking Applies to Education," Educational Leadership 50 (3), 38-41.

Bianchi, S. M. (1984). "Children's Progress Through School: A Research Note," Sociology of Education, 57, 184-192.

Blackman, B. (1983). "Are We Assessing the Linguistic Factors Critical in Early Reading?" Annals of Dyslexia, 33, 91-109.

Blackman, B. (1984). "The Relationships of Rapid Naming Ability and Language Analysis Skills to Kindergarten and First Grade Reading Achievement," Journal of Educational Psychology, 76, 10-22.

Block, J., and Burns, R. (1976). "Master Learning," Review of Research in Education, Vol. 4, edited by L. S. Shulman, Itasca, IL.: Peacock.

Bloom, B.S. (1976). Human Characteristics and School Learning. New York: McGraw Hill Evans, K. M. and King, J. A. (1994). "Research on OBE: What We Know and Don't Know," Educational Leadership, 51:6.

Bloom, B.S. (1984). "The Search for Methods of Group Instruction as Effective as One-to-One Tutoring". Educational Leadership, 41 (8), 4-17.

Blumenfeld, P., & Meece., J. (1988). "Task Factors, Teacher Behavior, and Students' Involvement and Use of Learning Strategies in Science," Elementary School Journal, 88, 235-250.

Blumenfeld, P., Soloway E., Marx, R., Krajcik, J., Guzdial, M., & Palcinsar, A. (1991). "Motivating Project-Based Learning: Sustaining the Doing, Supporting the Learning," Educational Psychologist, 26, 369-398.

Blyth, D. A., & Simmons, R. G. (1987). Moving Into Adolescence: The Impact of Pubertal Change and School Context. Hawthorne, N. Y.: Aldine De Gruyter.

Blyth, D. A., Simmons, R. G., & Carlton-Ford, S. (1983). "The Adjustment of Early Adolescents to School Transitions," Journal of Early Adolescence, 3; 105-120.

Boggiano, a. K., D. N. . Ruble, and T. S. Pittman. (1982). 'The Mastery Hypotheses and the Overjustification Effect," Social Cognition 1: 38-49.

Bonstingl, J. J. (1992). "The Quality Revolution in Education," Educational Leadership. 50, (3): 4-9.

Bower, E. M. (1969). Early Identification of Emotionally Handicapped Children in School. Springville, IL: Charles C. Thomas.

Braddock, J. H. . and Slavin, R. E. (1993). Life in the Slow Lane: A Longitudinal Study of Effects of Ability Grouping on Student Achievement, Attitudes, and Perceptions. Baltimore, MD: John Hopkins University, Center for Research on Effective Schooling for Disadvantaged Students.

Bradley, L. and Bryant, P. (1983). "Categorizing Sounds and Learning to Read - A Causal Connection," Nature, 301, 419-421.

Bradley, L. and Bryant, P. (1985). Rhyme and Reason in Reading and Spelling. Ann Arbor: University of Michigan Press.

Bradley, R. H. (1985). "Review of The Gesell School Readiness Test," In J. V. Mitchell, Jr. (Ed.), The Ninth Mental Measurements Yearbook (Vol. 1, pp. 609-610). Lincoln, NE: Buros Institute of Mental Measurements.

Brandt, R. (1992a). "On Outcome-Based Education: A Conversation with Bill Spady." Educational Leadership vol. 50 (4) , pp. 66-70.

Brandt, R. (1992b). "On Deming and School Quality: A Conversation With Enid Brown," Educational Leadership. 49, (6), 28-31.

Bransford, J. D., Sherwood, R., Vye, N., Reiser, J. (1986). "Teaching Thinking and Problem-Solving: Suggestions from Research," American Psychologist. 41, 1078-1089.

Bredekamp, S. (Ed.). (1987). Developmentally Appropriate Practices in Early Childhood Programs Serving Children from Birth Through Age Eight. Washington, DC: National Association for the Education of Young Children.

Brockman, M. A., & Reeves, A. W. (1967). "Relationship Between Transiency and Test Achievement," Alberta Journal of Educational Research, 13, 319-330.

Brodinsky, B and Keough, K. (1989). Students At Risk: Problems and Solutions. AASA Critical Issues Report. Arlington, Virginia: American Association of School Administrators.

Bronfenbrenner, U. (1974). The Ecology of Human Development. MA: Harvard University Press, 1974.

Bronfenbrenner, U. (1977). "Toward an Experimental Ecology of Human Development. American Psychologist, 32, 513-529.

Brook, J., Nomura, C. and Cohen, P. (1989). "A Network of Influences on Adolescent Drug Involvement: Neighborhood, School, Peer, and Family," Genetic, Social and General Psychology Monographs 115(1). 303-321.

Brookover, W. B., Beady, C. H., Flood, P. K. & Wisenbaker, J. M. (1978). "Elementary School Social Climate and School Achievement," American Educational Research Journal, 15(2), 301-318.

Brookover, W. B., Beady, C., Flood, P. Schweitzer, J. & Wisenbaker, J. (1977). Schools Can Make a Difference: A Study of Elementary School Social Systems and School Outcomes. Paper prepared for East Lansing: Michigan State University, Center for Urban Affairs.

Brophy , J. & McCaslin, M. (1992). "Teachers' Reports of How They Perceive and Cope with Problem Students," Elementary School Journal, 93, 3-68.

Brophy, J. & Evertson, C. (1976). Learning From Teaching: A Developmental Perspective. Boston: Allyn & Bacon.

Brophy, J. & Kher, N. (1986). "Teacher Socialization as a Mechanism for Developing Student Motivation to Learn," In R. Feldman (Ed.), Social Psychology Applied to Education. New York: Cambridge University Press.

Brophy, J. (1983). "Classroom Organization and Management," Elementary School Journal, 83, 265-285.

Brophy, J. (1983). "Conceptualizing Student Motivation," Educational Psychologist, 18, 200-215.

Brophy, J. (1988). "Educating Teachers About Managing Classrooms and Students," Teaching and Teacher Education, 4, 1-18.

Bulach, C. & Malone, B. (1994). "The Relationship of School Climate to the Implementation of School Reform," ERS Spectrum: Journal of School Research and Information. Vol.12, No. 4.

Butkowsky, I., and Willows, D. (1980). "Cognitive-Motivational Characteristics of Children Varying in Reading Ability: Evidence for Learned Helplessness in Poor Readers," Journal of Educational Psychology, 72, 408-482.

Butler, R. (1987). "Task-Involving and Ego-Involving Properties of Evaluation: Effects of Different Feedback Conditions on Motivational Perceptions, Interest, and Performance." Journal of Educational Psychology 79: 472-482.

Byrnes, D., & Yamamoto, K. (1986). "Views on Grade Repetition," Journal of Research and Development in Education, 20(1), 14-20.

Caine, R. N. and Caine, G. C. (1990). "Understanding a Brain-Based Approach to Learning and Teaching," Educational Leadership. Vol. 48 (2). pp. 66-70.

Caine, R. N. and Caine, G. C. (1991). Teaching and the Human Brain, Making Connections. Alexandria, VA.: ASCD.

California State Department of Education. (1986) The Problem/Scope of High Risk Youth. High Risk Youth Liaison and Field Services Unit.

Carrier, C. & Titus, A. (1979). "The Effects of Notetaking: A Review of Studies," Contemporary Educational Psychology, 4, 299-314.

Cates, W. M. and McNaull, P. A. and Gardner (1993). "Inservice Training and University Coursework: Its Influence on Computer Use and Attitudes Among Teachers of Learner Disabled Students," Journal of Research on Computing in Education, 25(4), 447-63.

Center for Education Statistics (1986). Public School Teacher Perspectives on School Discipline. Washington, D.C.: U.S. Department of Education.

Clark, R. (1983). Family Life and School Achievement: Why Poor Black Children Succeed or Fail. Chicago: University of Chicago Press.

Clay, M. M. (1985). The Early Detection of Reading Difficulties. Portsmouth, NH: Heinemann.

Coddington, R. D. (1972). "The Significance of Life Events as Etiologic Factors in Disease of Children - II. A Study of a Normal Population," Journal of Psychosomatic Research, 16, 205-213.

Coleman, J. S., Campbell, E. Q., Hobson, C. J., McPartland, J., Mood, A., Weinfeld, F. D. & York, R. L. (Eds.). (1966). Equality of Educational Opportunity. Washington, DC: U.S. Government Printing Office.

Combs, A. W., and Syngg, D. (1959). Individual Behavior: A Perceptual Approach to Behavior. New York: Harper & Row.

Condry, J., and Chambers, J. (1978). 'Intrinsic Motivation and the Process of Learning," In M. Lepper & D. Greene (Eds.). The Hidden Costs of Reward: New Perspectives on the Psychology of Human Motivation. Hillsdale, NJ: Erlbaum

Conrad, D., and Hedin, D. (1989). High School Community Service: A Review of Research and Programs. Madison, Wis.: National Center on Effective Secondary Schools.

Conrath, J. (1986). Our Other Youth. Gig Harbor, WA.

Conrath, J. (1987). As the Pendulum Swings: Four Cautions for Alternative Educators ED# 282938.

Conrath, J. (1988). "Dropout Prevention: Find Out if Your Program Passes or Fails. The Executive Educator 10-8:15-16. EJ 374 905.

Conrath, J. (1992). "Effective Schools for Discouraged and Disadvantaged Students: Rethinking Some Sacred Cows of Research," Contemporary Education. v63, n2, p137-141.

Contribute to the Problem," Teachers College Record 87 Spring:374-392.

Cooley W. W. , and Leinhardt, G. L. (1978). The Instructional Dimensions Study: The Search for Effective Classroom Processes: Final Report. Washington DC: National Institute of Education.

Cooper, H. (1979). "Pygmalion Grows Up: A Model for Teacher Expectation Communication and Performance Influence," Review of Educational Research, 49, 389-410.

Cooper, H. (1995) The Battle Over Homework: An Administrator's Guide to Setting Sound and Effective Policies. Thousand Oaks, CA: Corwin Press, Inc.

Cornille, T. A., Bayer, A. E., & Smyth, C. K. (1983). "Schools and Newcomers: A National Survey of Innovative Programs," Personnel and Guidance Journal, 62, 229-236.

Costello, E. J. (1989). Developments in Child Psychiatric Epidemiology: Introduction. Journal of the American Academy of Child and Adolescent Psychiatry, 28, 836-841.

Craske, N. (1988). "Learned Helplessness, Self-Worth Motivation and Attribution Retraining for Primary School Children," British Journal of Educational Psychology, 58, 152-164.

Crawford, J. (1989). "Instructional Activities Related to Achievement Gain in Chapter I Classes," In Slavin, R. E.; Karweit, N. L; and Madden, N. A. (Eds.) Effective Programs for Students At Risk. Boston: Allyn and Bacon.

Crockett, L. J., Petersen, A., Graber, J., Schulenberg, J. E., & Ebata, A. (1989). "School Transitions and Adjustment During Early Adolescence," Journal of Early Adolescence 9, 3:181-210.

Cuban, L. (1989). "The At-Risk Label and the Problem of Urban School Reform," Phi Delta Kappan, June.

Cullinan, D., & Epstein, H. (1986). "Behavior Disorders," In N. Haring (Ed.), Exceptional Children and Youth. (4th ed.). Columbus, OH: Merrill.

Cummins, J. 1984. Bilingualism and Special Education: Issues in Assessment and Pedagogy, San Diego, CA: College-Hill Press.

Curry, L. (1990), "A Critique of the Research on Learning Styles," Educational Leadership, 48(2), 15-21.

David, J. K., and P. M. Shields. (1991). From Effective Schools to Restructuring: A Literature Review. Menlo Park, CA: SRI International.

Davidson, N. (1985). "Small-Group Learning and Teaching in Mathematics: A Selective Review of the Research." In Learning to Cooperate, Cooperating To Learn. Edited by R. E. Slavin, S. Sharan, s. Kagan, R. Hertz-Lazarowitz, C. Webb, and R. Schmuck. pp. 221-230. New York: Plenum.

Davis, F. (1968). "Research in Comprehension in Reading," Reading Research

Davis, W. E. (1991). Promoting Effective Communication Between Schools and Parents of Disadvantaged Students. Paper Presented at the 99th Annual Convention of the American Psychological Association, San Francisco, CA.: Department of Education, National Center for Education Statistics.

deCharms, R. (1976). Enhancing Motivation: Change in the Classroom. New York: Irvington.

Deci, E., and Ryan, R. (1985). Intrinsic Motivation and Self-Determination in Human Behavior. New York: Plenum.

Demos, V. (1989). "Resiliency in Infancy," In Dugan, T. and Coles, R. (Eds.), The Child in Our Times. 3-22.

Dohrenwend, B. S. (1978). "Social Stress and Community Psychology," American Journal of Community Psychology, 6, 1-14.

Donmoyer, R. and Kos, R. (1993). "At-Risk Students: Insights From/About Research. In Donmoyer, R. and Kos., R. (Eds.), At-Risk Students Portraits, Policies, Programs, and Practices Albany, NY: State University of New York Press.

Doss, D., and Holley, F. (1982). A Cause for National Pause: Title I Schoolwide Projects. Paper presented at the annual meeting of the American Educational Research Association, New York.

Doyle, W. (1986). "Classroom Organization and Management," Handbook of Research on Teaching (3rd ed.). New York: Macmillan.

Doyle, W. (1990). "Classroom Management Techniques," In Moles, O. C. (Ed.), Student Discipline Strategies: Research and Practice. Albany, NY: State University of New York Press.

Dryfoos, J. (1990). Adolescents at Risk: Prevalence and Prevention. New York: Oxford University Press.

Dryfoos, J. G. (1987). Youth at Risk: One in Four in Jeopardy. Hastings-on-Hudson, NY: Carnegie Corporation.

Duckenfield, Ml, and Swanson, L. (1992). Service Learning. Meeting the Needs of Youth At Risk. Clemenson, SC: National Dropout Prevention Center.

Duke, D. L. & Perry, C. (1978). "Can Alternative Schools Succeed Where Benjamin Spock, Spiro Agnew, and B. F. Skinner Have Failed?" Adolescence. 13, 375-392.

Duke, D. L., (1990). "School Organization, Leadership, and Student Behavior," In Moles, O. C. (Ed.). Student Discipline Strategies: Research and Practice. New York, NY: State University of New York Press.

Dunn, R., Beaudry, J., and Klavas, A. (1989), "Survey of Research on Learning Styles," Educational Leadership, 46(6), 50-58.

Dweck, C., and Elliott, E. (1983). "Achievement Motivation," In P. Mussen (Ed.), Handbook of Child Psychology (4th ed.), Vol. IV: Socialization, Personality, and Social Development. New York: Wiley.

Dyer, P. (1992). "Reading Recovery: A Cost-Effectiveness and Educational-Outcomes Analysis," ERS Spectrum, 10, 10-19.

Eccles, J. S., Lord, S., & Midgley, C. (1991). "What Are We Doing to Early Adolescents? The Impact of Educational Contexts on Early Adolescents," American Journal of Education 99, 4: 521-542.

Eder, C. (1981). "Ability Grouping as a Self-Fulfilling Prophecy: A Micro-Analysis of Teacher-Student Interaction," Sociology of Education, 54, 151-162.

Edmonds, R. (1986). "Characteristics of Effective Schools," In The School Achievement of Minority Children: New Perspectives. Hillsdale, NJ: Lawrence Erlbaum, 93-104.

Education Week (May 14, 1986): 30.

Educational Research Newsletter.(1993) Vol. 6 (2); March/April.

Educational Research Service. (1978). Class Size: A Summary of Research. Arlington, VA: Educational Research Service.

Educational Resources Information Center (ERIC). (1987). Thesaurus of ERIC Descriptors. Phoenix. AZ: Oryz.

Ekstrom, R. B. .; Goertz, M.; Pollack, J.; Rock, D. (1986). "Who Drops Out of High School and Why? Findings From a National Study," Teachers College Record 87:356-373.

Elkind, D. (1981). The Hurried Child. Reading, MA: Addison-Wesley.

Ellis, A. K. , and Fouts, J. T. (1993). Research on Educational Innovations. Princeton Junction, NJ.: Eye on Education.

Emmer, E. & Aussiker, A. (1990). "School and Classroom Discipline Programs: How Well Do They Work?" In O. C. Moles (Ed.). Student discipline Strategies: Research and Practice. Albany: State University of New York Press.

Emmer, E., & Aussiker, A. (1987, April). School and Classroom Discipline Programs: How Well Do They Work? Paper presented at the annual meeting of the American Educational Research Association, Washington, DC.

Emmer, E., Evertson, C., & Anderson, L. (1979). Effective Classroom Management at the Beginning of the School Year. Austin: University of Texas, Research and Development Center for Teacher Education.

Engel, P. (1991). "Tracking Progress Toward the School Readiness Goal," Educational Leadership, 48(5), 39-42.

Englander, M. (1986). Strategies for Classroom Discipline. New York: Praeger.

Evertson, C., & Harris, A. (1992). "What We Know About Managing Classrooms," Educational Leadership, 49, 74-78.

Farrell, E. (1990). Hanging In and Dropping Out: Voices of At-Risk High School Students. New York: Teachers College Press.

Fay J. & Funk, D. (1995). Teaching With Love & Logic. Golden, CO: The Love and Logic Press Inc.

Feather, N. (Ed.). (1982). Expectations and Actions. Hillsdale, NJ: Erlbaum.

Feldman, R.; Stiffman, A.; and Jung, K. (1987). (Eds.) Children at Risk: In the Web of Parental Mental Illness. New Brunswick, NJ: Rutgers University Press.

Felner, R. D., Ginter, M. A., & Primavera, J. (1982). "Primary Prevention During School Transitions: Social Support and Environmental Structure," American Journal of Community Psychology, 10, 277-290.

Felner, R. D., Primavera, J., & Cauce, A.M. (1981). "The Impact of School Transitions: A Focus for Preventive Efforts," American Journal of Community Psychology 9, 4: 449-459.

Ferrell, B. G. (1983), " A Factor Analytic Comparison of Four Learning Styles Instruments", Journal of Educational Psychology, 75(1), 33-39.

Fields, J. C. (1993). Total Quality for Schools: A Suggestion for American Education. Milwaukee, Wisconsin: ASQC Quality Press.

Fine, M. (1986). "Why Urban Adolescents Drop Into and Out of Public High School," Teachers College Record 87 Spring:393-409

Fine, M. (1987). "Why Urban Adolescents Drop Into and Out of Public High School," School Dropout: Patterns and Policies. Gary Natriello (Ed.). New York: Teachers College Press.

Fine, M. (1991). Framing Dropouts: Notes on the Politics of an Urban Public High School. Albany, NY: State University of New York Press.

Folger, J. (1989). "Lessons for Class Size Policy and Research," Peabody Journal of Education Vol. 67, (1), p. 123-32.

Fowler, J. W., and Peterson, P. L. (1981). "Increasing Reading Persistence and Altering Attributional Style of Learned Helpless Children," Journal of Educational Psychology, 73, 251-260.

Fraser, M. (1974) Children in Conflict. Harmondsworth, England: Penguin books.

Frieze, I., Francis, W., and Hanusa, B. (1983). "Defining Success in Classroom Settings," In J. Levine and M. Wang (Eds.), Teacher and Student Perceptions: Implications for Learning. Hillsdale, NJ: Erlbaum.

Frymier, J. (1989). A Study of Students At Risk: Collaborating to do Research. (Phi Delta Kappa Monograph Series). Bloomington, IN: Phi Delta Kappa Educational Foundation.

Frymier, J. (1992). Growing Up Is Risky Business, and Schools Are Not to Blame. Bloomington, IN: Phi Delta Kappa

Frymier, J. and Gansneder, B. (1989). "The Phi Delta Kappa Study of Students At Risk. Phi Delta Kappan, 71(2), 142-146.

Gaa, J. P. (1973). "Effects of Individual Goal-Setting Conferences on Achievement, Attitudes, and Goal-Setting Behavior," Journal of Experimental Education 42: 22-28.

Gaa, J. P. (1979). "The Effects of Individual Goal-Setting Conferences on Achievement, Attitudes, and Modification of Locus of Control," Psychology in the Schools 16: 591-597.

Gallagher, J. J. . (1993). "Ability Grouping: A Tool for Educational Excellence," The College Board Review, No.168.

Gandara, P. (1982). "Passing Through the Eye of the Needle: High Achieving Chicanas," Hispanic Journal of Behavioral Sciences 4, no.2: 167-180.

Garbino, J. (1980). "Preventing Child Maltreatment," In Price, R. (Ed.) Prevention in Mental Health: Research, Policy, and Practice. Beverly Hills, CA: Sage.

Gardner, H. (1983). Frames of Mind. New York, NY: Basic Books.

Gardner, H. (1991). The Unschooled Mind: How Children Think and How Schools Should Teach. New York: Basic Books.

Garmezy, N. (1983). "Stressors of Childhood," In Garmezy, N. and Rutter, M. (Eds.) Stress, Coping and Development. New York: McGraw-Hill.

Gesell, A. (1940). The First Five Years of Life. New York: Harper & Brothers.

Gettinger, M. (1988). "Methods of Proactive Classroom Management," School Psychology Review, 17, 227-242.

Gickling, E. E. and Thompson, V. P. (1985). "A Personal View of Curriculum-Based Assessment," Exceptional Children, November, 1985.

Gilman, D. A. & Tillitsky, C. (1989). The Longitudinal Effect Size of Prime Time, Indiana's State Sponsored Reduced Class Size Program. Indiana State University: 2-5, 9-11.

Gilman, D. A. (1993). Small Classes: Miracle or Myth. Terre Haute Tribune-Star, 24 February: 1.

Glass, G., Cahen, L., Smith, M., & Filby, N. (1982). School Class Size: Research and Policy. Beverly Hills, CA: Sage.

Glasser, W. (1965). Reality Therapy. New York: Harper and Row.

Glasser, W. (1969). Schools Without Failure. New York: Harper and Row.

Glasser, W. (1988). "On Students' Needs and Team Learning: A Conversation With William Glasser," R. Brandt (Ed.), Educational Leadership, 45, 38-45.

Gnezda, M. T. and Bolig, R. (1988). A National Survey of Public School Testing of Pre-Kindergarten and Kindergarten Children Washington, D. C.: National Forum on the Future of Children and Families, National Research Council.

Goettler-Sopko, S. (1990). The Effect of Class Size on Reading Achievement. EDRS document: 325826.

Goldstein, S. (1995). Understanding and Managing Children's Classroom Behavior. New York, NY: John Wiley & Sons, Inc.

Good, T. L. & Brophy J. E. (1994). Looking in Classrooms. (6th ed.). New York, NY: Harper Collins College Publishers.

Goodlad, J. (1984). A Place Called School. New York: McGraw-Hill.

Gordon, T. (1974). T.E.T. Teacher Effectiveness Training. New York: McKay.

Graff, G. (1992). Beyond the Culture Wars: How Teaching the Conflicts Can Revitalize American Education. New York: Norton.

Graves, T. (1991). "The Controversy Over Group Rewards in Cooperative Classrooms," Educational Leadership 48 (7), 77-79.

Gredler, G. R. (1984). "Transition Classes: A Viable Alternative for the At-Risk Child?," Psychology in the Schools, 21, pp. 463-70.

Grissom, J. B., & Shepard, L. A. (1989). "Repeating and Dropping Out of School," In L. A. Shepard & M. L. Smith (Eds.), Flunking Grades: Research and Policies on Retention. (pp. 34-63). Philadelphia: Palmer Press.

Guskey, T. R., (1994). "What You Assess May Not Be What You Get," Educational Leadership. 51, 6:51-54.

Guskey, T. R., and Gates, S. L. (1986). "Syntheses of Research on the Effects of Mastery Learning in Elementary and Secondary Classrooms," Educational Leadership, 43,(8), 73-81.

Gutierrez, R. and Slavin, R.E. (1993). "Achievement Effects of the Nongraded Elementary School: A Best Evidence Syntheses," Review of Educational Research Vol. 62 (4), pp. 333-376.

Hall, D. P., Prevatte, C., & Cunningham, P. M. (1993). Elementary Ability Grouping and Failure in the Primary Grades. Unpublished manuscript.

Hallinan, M. (1987). "Ability Grouping and Student Learning," In M. Hallinan (Ed.), The Social Organization of Schools: New Conceptualizations of the Learning Process (pp.41-69). New York: Plenum Press.

Hargis, C. H.; Terhaar-Yonkers, M.; Williams, P.C.; and Reed, M. T. (1988). "Repetition Requirements for Word Recognition," Journal of Reading, 31, 320-327.

Hargis, C.H. (1989). Teaching Low Achieving and Disadvantaged Students. Springfield, IL: Thomas.

Hart, D. (1994). Authentic Assessment: A Handbook for Educators. Menlo Park, Calif.: Addison Wesley.

Hart, L. (1983). Human Brain, Human Learning. New York: Longman, Inc.

Heck, R. H. et al. (1990). "Instructional Leadership and School Achievement: Validation of a Causal Model," Educational Administration Quarterly Vol. 26, No. 2:94-126.

Heffernan, D. and Tarlov, S. (1989). Service Opportunities for Youths. Washington, DC: Children's Defense Fund.

Hembree, R. (1988). "Correlates, Causes, Effects, and Treatment of Test Anxiety," Review of Educational Research, 58, 47-77.

Hepler, N., Stringfield, S., Seltzer, D., Fortna, R., Stonehill, R., Yoder, N., & English, J. (1987). Effective Compensatory Education Programs for Extremely Disadvantaged Students. Portland, OR: Northwest Regional Educational Laboratory.

Herman, J. L. . (1992). "What Research Tells Us About Good Assessment," Educational Leadership. 49,8:74-78.
Heskin, K. (1980). Northern Ireland: A Psychological Analysis. New York: Columbia University Press.
Hiebert, E. and Taylor, B. (Eds.). (1994). Getting Ready Right From the Start: Effective Early Literacy Interventions. Needham Heights, MA: Allyn & Bacon.
Hiebert, E. H., Colt, J. M., Catto, S.L., & Gury, E. C. (1992). "Reading and Writing of First-Grade Students in a Restructured Chapter I Program," American Educational Research Journal, 29, 545-572.
Hill, K. T., and Wigfield, A. (1984). "Test Anxiety: A Major Educational Problem and What Can Be Done About It," Elementary School Journal, 85, 105-126.
Hodgkinson, H. (1994). The Demographics of Michigan: Implications for Educational Reform
Holdaway, D. (1979). The Foundations of Literacy. Sydney, Australia: Ashton
Holland, J. V., Kaplan, D. M., & Davis, S. D. (1974). "Inter-School Transfers: A Mental Health Challenge," Journal of School Health, 44, 74-79.
Holmes, C. T. & Mathews, K. M. (1984). "The Effects of Nonpromotion on Elementary and Junior High School Pupils: A Meta-Analysis," Review of Educational Research,54, 2, pp. 225-36.
Holmes, C. T. (1989). "Grade Level Retention Effects: A Meta-Analysis of Research Studies, " In Shepard, L. A. and Smith, M. L. (Eds.) Flunking Grades: Research and Policies on Retention. Philadelphia, PA: the Falmer Press.
Howe, H. (1985). "Giving Equity a Chance in the Excellence Game," In The Great School Debate: Which Way for American Education? edited by B. and R. Gross. NY: Simon and Schuster.
Hoyle, J. R., English, F. W., & Steffy, B. E. (1985). Skills for Successful School Leadership. Arlington, VA: The American Association of School Administrators.
Jason, L. A., Betts, D., Johnson, J. H., Smith, S., Krueckeberg, S., & Cradock, M. (1989). "An Evaluation of an Orientation Plus Tutoring School-Based Prevention Program," Professional School Psychology, 4, 273-284.
Jason, L. A., Betts, D., Johnson, J. H., Weine, A.M., Neuson, L., Filippelli, L., & Lardon, C. (1992b). "Developing, Implementing, and Evaluating Preventive Intervention for High Risk Transfer Children," In T. Kratochwill (Ed.), Advances in School Psychology (pp. 45-77). Hillsdale, NJ: Erlbaum.
Jason, L. A., Weine, A. M., Warren Sohlberg, L., Filippelli, L. A., Turner, E. Y., & Lardon, C. (1992a). Helping Transfer Students: Strategies for Educational and Social Readjustment. San Francisco, CA: Jossey-Bass.
Johnson, D. and Johnson, R. (1985). "Motivational Processes in Cooperative, Competitive, and Individualistic Learning Situations," In C. Ames and R. Ames (Eds.). Research on Motivation in Education. Vol. 2: The Classroom Milieu. Orlando, FL: Academic Press.
Johnson, D., Johnson R., and Holubec, E. (1990). Circles of Learning: Cooperation in the Classroom 3rd Ed. Edina, MN: Interaction Book Co.
Johnson, G. (1994). "An Ecological Framework for Conceptualizing Educational Risk," Urban Education April, 1994. pp.34-47.
Jones, V.F., & Jones, L. S. (1995). Comprehensive Classroom Management: Creating Positive Learning Environments for All Students. Boston, MA: Allyn and Bacon.
Karweit, N. (1983). Time on Task: A Research Review. (Report No. 332). Baltimore, MD: Center for the Social Organization of Schools.
Karweit, N. (1989). "Effective Kindergarten Programs and Practices for Students At Risk," In R. E. Slavin, N. Karweit, & N. A. Madden (Eds.), Effective Programs for Students At Risk. (pp. 103-142). Needham Heights, MA: Allyn and Bacon.
Karweit, N. (1992). "Synthesis of Research: the Kindergarten Experience," Educational Leadership, 49(6): 82-86.
Keefe, J. W. et al.(1985). "School Climate: Clear Definitions and a Model for a Larger Setting," NASSP Bulletin vol. 69, No. 484: 70-77.
Keller, J. (1983). "Motivational Design of Instruction," In C. Reigeluth (Ed.), Instructional-Design Theories and Models: An Overview of their Current Status. Hillsdale, NJ: Erlbaum.
Kelly, T. J. Bullock, C. M., & Dykes, M. K. (1977). Behavioral Disorders: Teachers' Perceptions. Exceptional Children, 43, 316-318.
Kembrough, J. and Hill, P.T. (1981). The Aggregate Effects of Federal Education Programs. Santa Monica, CA: Rand Corporation.
Kennedy, M. M., Birman, B. F. Demaline, R. E. (1986). The Effectiveness of Chapter I Services. Washington, DC: Office of Educational Research and Improvement, U. S. Department of Education.
Kierwa, K. (1985). "Investigating Notetaking and Review: A Depth of Processing Alternative," Educational Psychologist, 20, 23-32.

King, J. and Ladson-Billings, G. (1990). "The Teacher Education Challenge in Elite University Settings: Developing Critical Perspectives for Teaching in Democratic and Multicultural Societies," European Journal of Intercultural Education 1:15-20.

Kohn, A. (1990). "Effects of Rewards on Pro-Social Behavior." Cooperative Learning 10, 3: 23-24.

Kohn, A. (1991). "Group Grade Grubbing Versus Cooperative Learning." Educational Leadership 48: 5: 93-94.

Koretz, D; Linn, R.; Dunbar, S. and Shepard, L. (1991). The Effects of High Stakes Testing on Achievement. Presented at the annual meeting of the American Educational Research Association, Chicago.

Kounin, J. S. & Gump, P. (1961). "The Comparative Influence of Punitive and Non-Punitive Teachers Upon Children's Concept of School Misconduct," Journal of Educational Psychology, 52, 44-49.

Kounin, J. S. (1970). Discipline and Group Management in Classrooms. New York: Holt, Rinehart & Winston.

Kovale, K. A., and Forness, S. R. (1990). "Substance Over Style: Assessing the Efficacy of Modality Testing and Teaching," Exceptional Children, 54(4), 228-239.

Kozma, R. B. and Croninger, R. G. (1992) "Technology and the Fate of At-Risk Students," Education and Urban Society, Vol. 24 No. 4, 440-453.

Krasner, D. (1993). Risk and Protective Factors and Achievement of Children At Risk. Graduate School of Education, Los Angeles, California: University of California.

Kruglanski, A. (1978). "Endogenous Attribution and Intrinsic Motivation," In M. Lepper & D. Greene (Eds.). The Hidden Costs of Reward: New Perspectives on the Psychology of Human Motivation. Hillsdale, NJ: Erlbaum.

Kulik, C. L.C., & Kulik, J. A. (1991). "Effectiveness of Computer-Based Instruction: An Updated Analysis," Computers in Human Behavior, 7, 75-94.

Kulik, J. A. (1992). An Analysis of the Research on Ability Grouping: Historical and Contemporary Perspectives.. Report for Office of Educational research and Improvement. Washington, DC

Kulik, J. A. (1994). "Meta-Analytic studies of Findings on Computer-Based Instruction," In Technology Assessment in Education and Training. Baker, E. L. and O'Neil, H. F. Jr. (Eds).. Hillsdale, NJ: Erlbaum.

Lacey, C., & Blane, D. (1979). "Geographic Mobility and School Attainment: The Confounding Variables," Education Research, 21, 200-206.

Ladas, H. (1980). "Summarizing Research: A Case Study," Review of Educational Research, 50, 597-624.

Ladson-Billings, G. (1994). "What We Can Learn From Multicultural Education Research," Educational Research 51, 8:22-28.

Lakoff, G. (1987). Women, Fire and Dangerous Things. Chicago: The University of Chicago Press.

Lange, A. R. "More Findings on Homework," Education Quarterly Review 14: 13-17.

LAUSD Dropout Prevention/Recovery Committee.(1985). A Study of Student Dropout in the Los Angeles Unified School District. Summary presented to Dr. Harry Handler, Superintendent, and the Board of Education, Los Angeles, California.

Lehr, J. B.; Harris, H. W. (1988). At-Risk, Low-Achieving Students in the Classroom. Washington, DC: NEA Professional Library.

Leinhardt, G. L. , and Pallay, A. (1982). "Restrictive Educational Settings: Exile or Haven?" Review of Educational Research, 52, 557-578.

Lepper, M. (1983). "Extrinsic Reward and Intrinsic Motivation: Implications for the Classroom," In J. Levine & M. Wang (Eds.), Teacher and Student Perspectives: Implications for Learning. Hillsdale, NJ: Erlbaum.

Lepper, M. and Greene, D. (1978). The Hidden Costs of Reward. Hillsdale, NJ: Erlbaum.

Letgers, N. and Slavin, RE (1992). Elementary Students At Risk: A Status Report. Report No. 38 Center for Research on Effective Schooling for Disadvantaged Students, John Hopkins University. Baltimore, MD.

Lezotte, L. W., Hathaway, D.W., Miller, S.K., Passalacqua J., and Brookover, W.B. (1980). School Learning Climate and Student Achievement. Tallahassee, FL: the STA Center. 53.

Linn, R.; Baker, S.; Dunbar, S. (1991). "Complex, Performance-Based Assessment: Expectations and Validation Criteria," Educational Researcher 20,8:15-21.

Lipman, P. (1993). Teacher Ideology Toward African-American Students in Restructured Schools. Doctoral Diss.., University of Wisconsin-Madison.

Lock, E., and Latham, G. (1990). A Theory of Goal Setting and Task Performance. Englewood Cliffs, NJ: Prentice-Hall.

Lockwood, A. R. (1990). "High School Community Service: Research and Practice," NASSP Bulletin, May, 1990.

Long, L. (1975). "Does migration Interfere With Children's Progress in School?" Sociology of Education, 48, 368-381.

Madden, N. A., Slavin, R. E., Karweit, N. L., Dolan, L. J., & Wasik, B. A. (1991). "Success for All: Ending Reading Failure From the Beginning," Language Arts, 68, 47-52.

Madden, N. and Slavin, R. E. (1983). "Mainstreaming Students With Mild Handicaps: Academic and Social Outcomes," Review of Educational Research. 53. 519-569.
Malone, T., & Lepper, M. (1987). "Making Learning Fun: A Taxonomy of Intrinsic Motivation for Learning," In R. Snow & M. Farr (Eds.), Aptitude, Learning, and Instruction: III. Conative and Affective Process Analysis. Hillside, NJ: Erlbaum.
Mandel, H. P. and Marcus, S. I (1988). The Psychology of Underachievement: Differential Diagnosis and Differential Treatment. New York: John Wiley and Sons.
Mann, V. (1991). "Language Problems: A Key to Early Reading Problems," In B. Wong (Ed.). Learning About Learning Disabilities. (pp. 129-162). New York: Academic Press.
Manning, L. M. (1993). "Seven Essentials of Effective At-Risk Programs. The Clearing House Vol. 66, No. 3 135-138.
Mansfield, W., Alexander, D., & Farris, E. (1991). Teacher Survey on Safe, Disciplined, and Drug-Free Schools. Washington, DC: U.S. Department of Education, National Center for Educational Statistics.
Mantzicopoulos, P. and Morrison, D. (1992). "Kindergarten Retention: Academic and Behavioral Outcomes Through the End of Second Grade," American Educational Research Journal. Vol. 29, No. 1, pp. 182-198.
Marzano, R. J. (1994). "Lessons From the Field About Outcome-Based Performance Assessments," Educational Leadership 51, 6: 44-50.
Mason, J., & Allen, J. B. (1986). "A Review of Emergent Literacy With Implications for Research and Practice in Reading," In E. Z. Rothkipf (Ed.), Review of Research in Education 13 (pp. 3-47). Washington, DC: American Educational Research Association.
Mayer, R. (1979). "Can Advance Organizers Influence Meaningful Learning?" Review of Educational Research, 49, 371-383.
McCaslin, M. & Good, T. (1992). "Compliant Cognition: The Misalliance of Management and Instructional Goals in Current School Reform," Educational Researcher, 21, 4-17.
McGee, R., Feehan, M., Williams, S., Partridge, F., Silva, P.A., & Kelly, J. (1990). "DSM-III Disorders in a Large Sample of Adolescents," Journal of the American Academy of Child and Adolescent Psychiatry, 29, 611-619.
McMillan, J. H. and Reed, D. F. (1994). "At-Risk Students and Resiliency: Factors Contributing to Academic Success," The Clearing House January/February, p.137-140.
Means, B.; and Olson, K. (1994). "The Link Between Technology and Authentic Learning," Educational Leadership 51, 7:15-18.
Medway, D. M., and Venino, G. R. (1982). "The Effects of Effort Feedback and Performance Patterns on Children's Attribution and Task Persistence," Contemporary Educational Psychology, 7, 26-34.
Mehan, H., Hertweck, A., and Meihls, J. L. (1986). Handicapping the Handicapped. Palo Alto, CA: Stanford University Press.
Meisels, S. J. (1987). "Uses and Abuses of Developmental Screening and School Readiness Testing," Young Children, Vol. 42, pp. 4-6, 68-73.
Meisels, S. J. (1988). "Developmental Screening in Early Childhood: The Interaction of Research and Social Policy," In Annual Review of Public Health, Vol. 9, edited by L. Breslow, J. E. Fielding, and L. B. Lave. Palo Alto, CA: Annual Reviews.
Meisels, S. J. (1989a). "High-Stakes Testing in Kindergarten," Educational Leadership, Vol. 46(7), pp. 16-22.
Meisels, S. J. (1989b). "Can Developmental Screening Tests Identify Children Who Are Developmentally at Risk?" Pediatrics, 83.
Mendler, A. (1992). What Do I Do When. . . ? How to Achieve Discipline With Dignity in the Classroom. Bloomington, IN: National Educational Services.
Mensch, E., & Mensch, H. (1991). The IQ Mythology: Class, Race, Gender and Inequality. Carbondale: Southern Illinois University Press.
Metz, M. H. (1978). Classroom and Corridors: The Crisis of Authority in Desegregated Secondary Schools. Berkeley: University of California Press.
Meyer, L. (1985). A Look at Instruction in Kindergarten: Observations of Interactions in Three School Districts. ED 268 489.
Michigan Department of Education, (1992). Early Childhood Standards of Quality: For PreKindergarten Through Second Grade. Document prepared for the Michigan Department of Education by the Ad Hoc Advisory Committee for Early Childhood Standards of Quality.
Miller, A. and Ohlin, L. (1985). Delinquency and Community: Creating Opportunities and Controls. Beverly Hills, CA: Sage.

Mitchell, D. E. and Beach, S. A. (1990). How Changing Class size Affects Classrooms and Students Policy Brief for US Department of Education. ED#: 358077.

Mitchell, R. (1992). Testing for Learning: How New Approaches to Evaluation Can Improve American Schools. New York: The Free Press.

Mizell, M. H. (1979). "Designing and Implementing Effective In-School Alternative to Suspension," In A. Garaboldi (Ed.), In-School Alternatives to Suspension. Washington, DC: National Institute of Education, U.S. Government Printing Office.

Moles, O. C. (Ed.) (1990). Student Discipline Strategies: Research and Practice: New York, NY: State University of New York Press.

Morgan, M. (1984). "Reward-Induced Decrements and Increments in Intrinsic Motivation." Review of Educational Research 54: 5-30.

Morphat, M. V., & Washburne, C. (1931). "When Should Children Begin to Read?" Elementary School Journal, 31, 496-503.

Morrow, L. M. (1989). Literacy Development in the Early Years: Helping Children Read and Write. Englewood Cliffs, NJ: Prentice-Hall.

Morrow, L. M. (1992). "The Impact of a Literature-Based Program on Literacy Achievement, Use of Literature, and Attitudes of Children From Minority Backgrounds," Reading Research Quarterly, 27, 250-275.

Morrow, L. M. and Rand, M. K. (1993). "Preparing Teachers to Support the Literacy Development of Young Children," (pp. 178-195). In Spodek, B. and Saracho, O. (Eds.). Language and Literacy in Early Childhood Education. New York: Teachers College Press.

Mortimore, P., & Sammons, P. (1987). "New Evidence on Effective Elementary Schools," Educational Leadership, 45, 4-8.

Moskovitz, S. (1983) Love Despite Hate: Child Survivors of the Holocaust and Their Adult Lives. New York: Schocken.

Muller, C. (1991b). "Working Mothers: the Effect of Maternal Employment on the Eighth Grade Child," in Parents, Children, and Schools. Chicago: National Opinion Research Center and National Center for Educational Statistics.

Muller, C.; Schiller, K; and Lee, S. (1991a). Defying Statistics or "Latch-Key Children in the Late '80s: Family Composition, Working Mothers, and After School Supervision." Paper presented at the Annual Meeting of the American Educational Research Association.

Myers, D.E., Milne, A. M. Baker, K., and Ginsburg, A. (1987). "Student discipline and High School Performance," Sociology of Education, 60, 18-33.

Nadel, L., and Wilmer, J. (1980). "Context and Conditioning: A Place for Space.: Physiological Psychology 8: 218-228.

NAEYC (1991). "Guidelines for Appropriate Curriculum Content and Assessment in Programs Serving Children Ages 3 Through 8," Young Children, Vol. 46, pp. 21-38.

Natriello, G. (1987). School Dropouts Patterns and Policies. New York, New York: Teachers College Press.

Natriello, G.; McDill E. L. ; Pallas, A. M. (1990). Schooling Disadvantaged Children Racing Against Catastrophe. New York, NY: Teachers College Press.

Naveh-Benjamin, M. (1991). "A Comparison of Training Programs Intended For Different Types of Test-Anxious Students: Further Support for an Information-Processing Model," Journal of Educational Psychology, 77, 623-630.

Newman, F. M. and Thompson, J. (1987). Effects of Cooperative Learning on Achievement in Secondary Schools: A Summary of Research. Madison, Wis.: University of Wisconsin, National Center on Effective Secondary Schools.

O'Connor, P. (1985). "Dropout Prevention Programs That Work," OSSC Bulletin, 29(4), 214-219.

O'Keefe, J., and Nadel, L. (1978). The Hippocampus as a Cognitive Map. Oxford: Clarendon Press.

O'Neil, J. (1990). "Making Sense of Style," Educational Leadership, 48(2), 4-9.

O'Neil, J. (1991). "Transforming the Curriculum for Students At Risk," ASCD Update, June.

Ogle, D. (1986). "K-W-L: A Teaching Model That Develops Active Reading of Expository Text," Reading Teacher, 39, 564-570.

Ornstein, R., and Sobel, D. (1987). The Healing Brain. New York: Simon and Schuster, Inc.

Pallardy, J. M. (1995). "Another Look at Homework," Principal, v.74 n.5, p. 32-33.

Pallas, A. (1991)."Who is at Risk? Definitions, Demographics, and Decisions," In Schwartz, W. and Howley, C. (Eds.), Overcoming Risk: an Annotated Bibliography of Publications Developed by ERIC Clearinghouses. Charleston, WV: ERIC Clearinghouse on Urban Education.

Panagos, J. L., Holmes, R. L., Thurman, R. L., Yard, G. J., & Spaner, S. D. (1981). "Operation Sail. One Effective Model for the Assimilation of New Students Into a School District," Urban Education, 15, 451-468.

Pasternak, C. S. (1986). Why Isn't Johnny in School? Effective Strategies for Attendance Improvement and Truancy Prevention. Tri-County Dropout Prevention Program, Grundy-Kendall Educational Service Region, Illinois.

Pavan, B. N. (1992). "The Benefits of Nongraded Schools," Educational Leadership Vol. 50 (2), pp.22-25.

Payne, B. D. , and Payne, D.A. (1989). "Sex, Race, and Grade Differences in the Locus of Control Orientations of At-Risk Elementary Students," Psychology in the Schools. Vol. 26, p.84-88.

Peck, K. L.; and Dorricott, D.(1994). "Why Use Technology?" Educational Leadership, 51, 7:11-14.

Peng, S. S. and R. T. . Takai. (1983). High School Dropouts: Descriptive Information from High School and Beyond. Washington DC: National Center for Education Statistics.

Peters, T. J. and Waterman, Jr. R. H. (1982). In Search of Excellence: Lessons from America's Best Run Companies. New York: Harper & Row.

Phinney, J. S. and Rotheram, M. J. eds. (1987). Children's Ethnic Socialization: Pluralism and Development. Beverly Hills, Calif.: Sage Publications.

Pikulski, J. J. (1994). "Preventing Reading Failure: A Review of Five Effective Programs," The Reading Teacher. Vol.48, No.1.

Pinnell, G. S. (1989). "Reading Recovery: Helping At-Risk children Learn To Read," The Elementary School Journal, 90, 161-183.

Pinnell, G. S., Fried, M.D., & Estice, R.M. (1990). "Reading Recovery: Learning How to Make a Difference,: The Reading Teacher, 43, 282-295.

Quality Education for Minorities Project: (1990). Education that works: an Action Plan for the Education of Minorities. Cambridge, Massachusetts Institute of Technology.

Raffini, J. P. (1988). Student Apathy: The Protection of Self-Worth. What Research Says to Teachers Series. Washington, DC: National Educational Association.

Reed, L.C. (1993). "Achieving the Aims and Purposes of Schooling Through Authentic Assessment," Middle School Journal. Nov., pp. 11-13.

Resnick, L. B. (1985). "Cognition and Instruction: Recent Theories of Human Competence," Master Lecture Series: vol. 4, Psychology and Learning, edited by B. L. . Hammonds. Washington, DC: American Psychological Association.

Resnick, L. B. (1987). Education and Learning To Think. Washington, D.C.: National Academy Press.

Reynolds, A. J. (1991). "Early Schooling of Children At Risk," American Educational Research Journal, 28, 392-422.

Rice, W. K., Toles, R. E., Schulz, E. M., Harvey, J. T. and Foster, D. L. (1987). "A Longitudinal Investigation of Effectiveness of Increased Promotion Standards at Eighth Grade on High School Graduation," Paper presented at the annual meeting of the American Educational Research Association, Washington, DC, April.

Richardson, V.; Casanova, U. Placier, P.; Guilfoyle, K. (1989). School Children At-Risk. Philadelphia, PA: The Falmer Press.

Riebin, R. A., & Balow, B. (1978). "Prevalence of Teacher Identified Behavior Problems: A Longitudinal Study," Exceptional Children, 45, 102-111.

Robinson, G., & Wittebols, J. (1986). Class Size Research: A Related Cluster Analysis for Decision-Making. Arlington, VA: Educational Research Service.

Roderick, M. (1993). The Path to Dropping Out: Evidence for Intervention. Westport, Connecticut: Auburn House.

Rohrkemper, M. and Corno, L. (1988). "Success and Failure on Classroom Tasks: Adaptive Learning and Classroom Teaching," Elementary School Journal, 88, 297-312.

Rosenblatt, R. (1983). Children of War. Garden City, N.Y.: Anchor Press.

Rosenfield, I. (1988). The Invention of Memory. New York: Basic Books, Inc.

Rotberg, I. C. and Harvey, J. J. (1993). Federal Policy Options for Improving the Education of Low-Income Students. Volume 1 Findings and Recommendations. Institute on Education and Training. RAND.

Rumberger, R. W. . (1983). "Dropping Out of High School: the Influence of Race, Sex, and Family Background," American Educational Research Journal, 20.

Rutter, M. (1984). "Resilient Children," Psychology Today March, 57-65.

Rutter, M., Tizard, J. and Whitmore, K., eds. (1970). Education, Health, and Behavior. London: Longman.

Rutter, M.; Maughan, B.; Motimore, P.; Ouston, J.; & Smith, A. (1979). Fifteen Thousand Hours. Cambridge, MA: Harvard University Press.

Ryan, A. W. (1991). "Meta-Analysis of Achievement Effects of Microcomputer Applications in Elementary Schools," Educational Administration Quarterly, 27(2), 161-184.

Ryan, R. M. (1982). "Control and Information in the Intrapersonal Sphere: An Extension of Cognitive Evaluation Theory," Journal of Personality and Social Psychology 43: 450-461.

Sabatino, A. C. (1983). "Discipline: A National Issue," In D. A. Sabatino, A. C. Sabatino, & L. Mann (Eds.), Discipline and Behavioral Management. Rockville, MD: Aspen.

Sagor, R. (1993). At-Risk Students Reaching and Teaching Them. Massachusetts: Watersun Publishing Company, Inc.

San Diego City Schools Planning, Research, and Evaluation Division. (1985). The 1982-83 School Leaver Study of the San Diego Unified School District. Prepared by Robert Barr, San Diego, California: San Diego City Schools Planning, Research, and Evaluation Division.

Sartain, H. E. (1989) Nonachieving Students At Risk: School, Family and Community Intervention. Washington, DC: National Education Association.

Schaller, J. (1975). "The Relation Between Geographic Mobility and School Behavior," Man-Environment Systems, 5, 185-187.

Schlesinger, A. M. (1991). The Disuniting of America: Reflections on a Multicultural Society Knoxville, Tenn.: Whittle Direct Books.

Schmidt, M., Weinstein, T., Niemiec, R., & Walberg, H. J. (1985). Computer-Assisted Instruction With Exceptional Children: A Meta-Analysis of Research Findings. Paper presented at the annual meeting of the American educational Research Association, Chicago.

Schulenber, J. E., Asp, C. E., & Petersen, A. C. (1984) "School for the Young Adolescent's Perspective: A Descriptive Report." Journal of Early Adolescence 4, 2:107-130.

Schulz, E. M. et al. (1986). The Association of Dropout Rates With Student Attributes. Paper presented at the Annual Meeting of the American Educational Research Association. 67th, San Francisco, CA.

Schunk, D. (1984). "Sequential Attributional Feedback and Children's Achievement Behavior," Journal of Educational Psychology 76:1159-1169.

Schunk, D. (1991). "Self-Efficacy and Academic Motivation," Educational Psychology, 26, 207-231.

Schunk, D. H., and Hanson, A. R. (1985). "Peer Models: Influence on Children's Self-Efficacy and Achievement," Journal of Educational Psychology, 77, 313-322.

Schwartz, J. L.. and Viator, K. A. . Eds. (1990). The Prices of Secrecy: The Social, Intellectual, and Psychological Costs of Current Assessment Practices. Cambridge, MA: Educational Technology Center.

Senge, P. (1990). The Fifth Discipline: The Art & Practice of the Learning Organization. New York: Doubleday.

Shannon, P.. (1983). "The Use of Commercial Reading Materials in American Elementary Schools," Reading Research Quarterly, 19, 68-65.

Shavelson, R. J. ., and Stern, P. (1981). "Research on Teachers' Pedagogical Thoughts, Judgments, Decisions, and Behavior," Review of Educational Research, 51, 455-498.

Shavelson, R. J. .; Gao, X.; Baxter, G. R. . (1993). Sampling Variability of Performance Assessments. (CSE Technical report 361). Santa Barbara, Calif.: National Center for Research in Evaluation, Standards and Student Testing, UCLA.

Shepard, L. A. (1987). "The New Push for Excellence: Widening the Schism Between Regular and Special Education," Exceptional Children, 53, 327-329.

Shepard, L. A. (1989b). "A Review of Research on Kindergarten Retention," in Lorrie A. Shepard and Mary Lee Smith, eds., Flunking Grades; Research and Policies on Retention London: Falmer Press, pp. 64-78.

Shepard, L. A. (1994). "The Challenges of Assessing Young Children Appropriately," Phi Delta Kappan Vol. 76(3), pp.206-212.

Shepard, L. A. , and Smith, M. C. (1983). "An Evaluation of the Identification of Learning Disabled Students in Colorado," Learning Disability Quarterly, 6, 115-127.

Shepard, L. A. and Grau, M. E. (1993). "The Morass of School Readiness Screening: Research on Test Use and Test Validity," In Bernard Spodek, ed., Handbook of Research on the Education of Young Children New York: Macmillan. pp. 293-305.

Shepard, L. A. and Smith, M. C. (1985). Boulder Valley Kindergarten Study: Retention Practices and Retention Effects. Boulder, CO: Boulder Valley Public Schools.

Shepard, L. A. and Smith, M. C. (1986). "Synthesis of Research on School Readiness and Kindergarten Retention," Educational Leadership 44: 78-86.

Shephard, L. A. (1989a). "Why We Need Better Assessments," Educational Leadership 46, 7:4-9.

Shephard, L. A., & Smith, M. L. (Eds.) (1989). Flunking Grades: Research and Policies on Retention. Philadelphia: Falmer/Taylor & Francis Group.

Shin, M. R.; Tindal, G. A. ; Spira, D.; and Marston, D. (1987). "Practice of Learning Disabilities as Social Policy," Learning Disability Quarterly, 10, 17-28.

Short, P. M. (1988). "Effectively Disciplined Schools: Three Themes From Research," NASSP Bulletin, 72(504), 1-3.

Short, P. M., Short, R. J. & Blanton, C., (1994). Rethinking Student Discipline: Alternatives That Work. Thousand Oaks, CA: Corwin Press, Inc.

Silcox, H. (1993). "School-Based Community Service Programs-An Imperative for Effective Schools," NASSP Bulletin. February, 1993.

Silvernail, D. L. (1985). Developing Positive Student Self-Concept. Analysis and Action Series. Washington, D. C. : National Education Association.

Skiba, R.J., McLeskey, J., Waldron, N. L., & Grizzle, K. (1993). "The Context of Failure in the Primary Grades: Risk Factors in Low and High Referral Rate Classrooms. School Psychology Quarterly, 8, 81-98.

Slavin, R. E. (1983). Cooperative Learning. New York: Longman.

Slavin, R. E. (1986). Educational Psychology: Theory Into Practice. Englewood Cliffs, N.J.: Prentice-Hall.

Slavin, R. E. (1988). "Cooperative Learning and Student Achievement," Educational Leadership 45, 2:31-33.

Slavin, R. E. (1989/90). "Research on Cooperative Learning: Consensus and Controversy," Educational Leadership, 47(4), 52-54.

Slavin, R. E. (1990a). Cooperative Learning: Theory, Research, and Practice. Englewood, NJ: Prentice-Hall.

Slavin, R. E. (1990b). "Class Size and Student Achievement: Is Smaller Better?". Contemporary Education, 62, pp. 6 - 12.

Slavin, R. E. (1991a). "Synthesis of Research on Cooperative Learning,: Educational Leadership, 48(5), 71-82.

Slavin, R. E. (1991b). "Group Rewards Make Groupwork Work," Educational Leadership, 48 (5): 89-91.

Slavin, R. E., and Braddock III, J. H. (1993). "Ability Grouping: On the Wrong Track," The College Board Review, No. 168.

Slavin, R. E., Madden, N. L., Karweit, N. L., Dolan, L., & Wasik, B. A. (1992). Success for All: A Relentless Approach to Prevention and Early Intervention in Elementary Schools. Arlington, VA: Educational Research Service.

Slavin, R.E. (1989). "Students At-Risk of School Failure: The Problem and its Dimensions," In R. E. Slavin, N. L. Karweit, & N. A. Madden (Eds.), Effective Programs for Students At Risk. (pp. 3-23). Boston: Allyn & Bacon.

Smey-Richman, B. & Barkley, W. W. (1991). Resources, Strategies, and Programs for Low-Achieving Students. School Climate Resource Document Prepared for the Office of Educational Research and Improvement. Philadelphia, PA: Research for Better Schools, Inc.

Smith, B. J. & Strain, P. S. (1988). Does Early Intervention Help? Reston, VA: Council for Exceptional Children.

Smith, F. (1983). "A Metaphor for Literacy: Creating Words or Shunting Information?" In F. Smith (Ed.), Essays Into Literacy (pp. 117-134). Exeter, NH: Heinemann.

Smith, M. L. (1983). How Educators Decide Who Is Learning Disabled. Springfield, IL: Charles C. Thomas Publishing.

Snow, C. E. and Perlmann, R. (1985). "Assessing Children's Knowledge About Book-Reading," In L. Galda & A. Pellegrini (Eds.), Play, Language, and Stories (pp. 167-181). Norwood, NJ: Ablex.

Snow, C. E. and Tabors, P. O. (1993). "Language Skills That Relate to Literacy Development," In Spodek, B. and Saracho, O. N. (Eds.). Language and Literacy in Early Childhood Education. New York: Teachers College Press.

Southern Regional Education Board, Atlanta, GA. (1994). Getting Schools Ready for Children: The Other Side of the Readiness Goal. Atlanta, GA: Southern Regional Education Board.

SPA. (1993). K-12 Market Study Report. Software Publishers Association.

Spodek, B. and Saracho, O. N (1993). Language and Literacy in Early Childhood Education. New York: Teachers College Press.

Stanovick, K. E. (1986). "Mathew Effects in Reading: Some Consequences of Individual Differences in the Acquisition of Literacy," Reading Research Quarterly, 21, 360-407.

Stedman, L. C. (1985, October). "A New Look at the Effective Schools Literature," Urban Education, 20, 295-326.

Stein, M. D. , Leinhardt, G. and Bickel, W. (1989). "Instructional Issues for Teaching Students At Risk." In Slavin, Robert E., Karweit, Karen L., and Madden, Karen A. (Eds): Effective Programs for Students at Risk. Boston, MA: Allyn and Bacon.

Steinberg, L.; Blinde, P. L. ; Chan, K. S. (1982) Dropping Out Among Language Minority Youth: A Review of the Literature. Los Alamitos, California: National Center for Bilingual Research.

Stern, D. (1986) Dropout Prevention and Recovery in California. Berkeley, California: University of California..

Sternberg, R. (1990). Metaphos of Mind: Conceptions of the Nature of Intelligence, New York: Cambridge University Press.

Sternberg, R. J., and Bhana, K. (1986). "Synthesis of Research on the Effectiveness of Intellectual Skills Programs: Snake-oil Remedy or Miracle Cures?" Educational Leadership, 44 (2), 60-67.

Stickard, J. and Mayberry, M. (1986). The Relationship Between School Environments and Student Achievement: A Review of Literature. R & D Center for Educational Policy and Management, College of Education, University of Oregon. 39.

Stipek, D., and Weisz, J. (1981). "Perceived Personal Control and Academic Achievement," Review of Educational Research, 51, 101-137.

Strickland, D. S. & Morrow, L. M. (Eds.). (1989). Emerging Literacy: Young Children Learn to Read and Write. Newark, DE: International Reading Association.

Strickland, D. S. (1990). "Emergent Literacy: How Young Children Learn to Read," Educational Leadership,(pp. 18-23).

Stringfield, S. and Yoder, N. (1992). "Toward a Model of Elementary Grades Chapter I Effectiveness," In Waxman, H. C., Walker de Felix, J., Anderson, J. E., Baptiste, Jr. H. P. (Eds.) Students at Risk in At-Risk Schools. Newbury Park, CA: Corwin Press, Inc.

Stringfield, S., Yoder, N. and Quilling, M. (1989). Effective Compensatory Education Programs for Extremely Disadvantaged Students. Paper presented at the American Educational Research Association, San Francisco.

Strong, J. H. and Jones, C. W. (1991). "Middle School Climate: The Principal's Role in Influencing Effectiveness," Middle School Journal Vol. 22, No. 5: 41-44.

Sulzby, E. (1991). "The Development of Prekindergarten Children and the Emergence of Literacy," In J. Flood, J. Jensen, d. Lapp, & J. R. Squire (Eds.), The Handbook of Research in the Teaching of the English Language Arts (pp. 273-285). New York: Macmillan.

Sulzby, E. and Edwards, P. A. "The Role of Parents in Supporting Literacy Development of Young Children," In Spodek, B. and Saracho, O. N. Language and Literacy in Early Childhood Education. New York: New Teachers Press.

Swanson, M. S. (1991). At-Risk Students in Elementary Education: Effective Schools for Disadvantaged Learners. Springfield, Illinois: Charles C. Thomas Publisher.

Sylwester, R. (1994). "What the Biology of the Brain Tells Us About Learning," Educational Leadership. Vol. 51 (4). pp.46-51.

Sylwester, R. (1995). A Celebration of Neurons: An Educators Guide to the Human Brain," Alexandria, VA: Association for Supervision and Curriculum Development (ASCD)

Sykora, R. J. (1981). "In-School Suspension - Alternatives Within An Option," NASSP Bulletin, 65(441), 119-122.

Taylor, B. M., Frye, B. J., Short, R., & Shearer, B. (1992). "Classroom Teachers Prevent Reading Failure Among Low-Achieving First-Grade Students," The Reading Teacher, 45, 592-597.

Taylor, B. M., Strait, J., & Meddo, M. A. (1994). "Early Intervention in Reading: Supplementary Instruction for Groups of Low Achieving Students Provided by First Grade Teachers," In E. H. Hiebert & B. M. Taylor (Eds.), Getting Reading Right From the Start: Effective Early Literacy Interventions. (pp. 107-121). Needham Heights, MA: Allyn & Bacon.

Teale, W. H., & Sulzby, E. (1986). "Emergent Literacy: A Perspective for Examining How Young Children Become Writers and Readers," In W. H. Teale & E. Sulzby (Eds.), Emergent Literacy: Writing and Reading (pp. iv-xxv). Norwood, NJ: Ablex.

Teale, W. H., & Sulzby, E. (1989). "Emergent Literacy: New Perspectives," In D. S. Strickland and L. M. Morrow (Eds.). Emerging Literacy: Young Children Learn to Read and Write. (pp. 1-15). Newark, Del.: International Reading Association

Thomas, J. W. (1980). "Perceived Personal Control and Academic Achievement," Review of Educational Research, 51, 101-137.

Thurstone, L. (1946). "A Note on a Reanalysis of Davis' Reading Tests," Psychometrika, 11, 185-188.

Tidwell, R. (1988). "Dropouts Speak Out: Qualitative Data on Early School Departures. Adolescence 23,92.

Tinto, V. (1987). Leaving College: Rethinking the Causes and Cures of Student Attrition. Chicago, Ill.: University of Chicago Press.

Tobias, S. (1989). "Tracked to Fail," Psychology Today, September, 1989.

Toby, J. & Scrupski, A. (1990). "Coerced Community Service as a School Discipline Strategy," In Moles, O. C. (Ed.) Student Discipline Strategies: Research and Practice. Albany, NY: State University of New York Press.

Tollefson, N., Tracy, D., Johnsen, E., Farmer, W., & Buenning, M. (1984). "Goal Setting and Personal Responsibility for LD Adolescents," Psychology in the Schools, 21, 224-233.

Tomlinson, T. M. (1990). "Class Size and Public Policy: The Plot Thickens," Contemporary Education, Vol. 62, (1).

Tomlinson, T. M. and Cross, C. T. (1991). "Student Effort: The Key to Higher Standards," Educational Leadership, 49 (1): 69-73.

Trueba, H. T. (1988). "Culturally Based Explanations of Minority Students' Academic Achievement," Anthropology and Education Quarterly, 19:270-287.

Tucker, J. A.. (1985). "Curriculum-Based Assessment: An Introduction," Exceptional Children, November, 1985.

U.S. Department of Education. (1993). Reinventing Chapter 1: Final Report of the National Assessment of the Chapter 1 Program. Washington, D.C.: U.S. Department of Education, Office of Policy and Planning.

Underwood, S., & Lumsden, L. S. (1994). "Class Size," Research Roundup. V11. (1).

Vandegrift, J. A. and Sandler, L. Linking Community Service and At-Risk Education. Briefing paper done for Arizona Serve-America Program. Tempe, AZ: Morrison Institute for Public Policy; Arizona State University.

Vasta, R.; Andrews, C. E.; McLaughlin, A. M.; Stirpe, L. A. and Comfort, C. (1978). "Reinforcement Effects on Intrinsic Interest: A Classroom Analog," Journal of School Psychology 16: 161-166.

Vellutino, F. R., & Scanlon, D. M. (1987). "Phonological Coding, Phonological Awareness, and Reading Ability: Evidence From Longitudinal and Experimental Study," Merrill-Palmer Quarterly, 33, 321-363.

Vyskocil, J. R. & Goens, G. A. (1979). "Collective Bargaining and Supervision: A Matter of Climate," Educational Leadership, 37 (1), 175-177.

Wallace, B., & Graves, W. (1995). Poisoned Apple: The Bell-Curve Crisis and How Our Schools Create Mediocrity and Failure. New York, NY: St. Martin's Press.

Wallerstein, J. S. and Kelly, J. B. (1980). Surviving the Breakup: How Children and Parents Cope with Divorce. New York: Basic Books.

Wasik, B. A., & Slavin, R. E. (1993). "Preventing Early Reading Failure With One-To-One Tutoring: A Review of Five Programs," Reading Research Quarterly, 28, 178-200.

Waters, E. (1985). Review of The Gesell Readiness Test. In J. V. Mitchell, Jr. (Ed.), The Ninth Mental Measurements Yearbook Vol.1, pp. 610-611. Lincoln, NE: Buros Institute of Mental Measurements.

Watt, N. et al. (1984). Children At-Risk for Schizophrenia: A Longitudinal Perspective. New York: Cambridge University Press.

Wayson, W. & Pinnell, G. (1982). "Creating a Living Curriculum for Teaching Self-Discipline," In D. Duke (Ed.), Helping Teachers Manage Classrooms. Alexandria, VA: Association for Supervision and Curriculum Development.

Webb, N. (1985). "Student Interaction and Learning in Small Groups: A Research Summary," Learning to Cooperate, Cooperating to Learn. Slavin, R.; Sharan, S.; Kagan, S.; Hertz-Lazarowitz, R; Webb, C. and Schmuck, R.; (Editors). New York: Plenum.

Weber, G. (1971). Inner City Children Can Be Taught To Read: Four Successful Schools. (Occasional paper 18). Washington, DC: Council for Basic Education.

Weber, J. M. and Silvani-Lacey, C. (1983). Building Basic Skills: The Dropout. Columbus, Ohio: The National Center for Research in Vocational Education, Ohio State University.

Wehlage, G. (1983). Effective Programs for the Marginal High School Student. Bloomington, Ind: Phi Delta Kappa.

Wehlage, G. G. .; Rutter, R. A. .; Smith, G.; Lesko, N.; Fernandez, R. (1989). Reducing the Risk: Schools as communities of Support. Philadelphia, Pa.: Falmer Press.

Wehlage, G. G. .; Rutter, R. A.; (1986). "Dropping Out: How Much Do Schools

Wehlage, G.; Rutter, R.; Smith, G.; Lesko, N.; & Fernandez, R. (1989). Reducing the Risk: Schools as Communities of Support. Philadelphia, PA: Falmer Press.

Weiner, B. (1992). Human Motivation: Metaphors, Theories and Research. Newbury Park, CA: Sage.

Weiner, B. and Kukla, A. (1970). "An Attributional Analysis of Achievement Motivation," Journal of Personality and Social Psychology 15:1-20.

Weinstein, R. S. (1976). "Reading Group Membership in First Grade: Teacher Behaviors and Pupil Experience Over Time," Journal of Educational Psychology, 68, 103-116.

Weisz, J., and Cameron, A. (1985). "Individual Differences in Students' Sense of Control," In C. Ames & R. Ames (Eds.), Research on Motivation in Education. Vol. 2: The Classroom Milieu. Orlando, FL: Academic Press.

Wells, S. (1990). At-Risk Youth: Identification, Programs, and Recommendations. Englewood, Colorado: Teacher Ideas Press.

Werner, E. (1984). Child Care: Kith, Kin and Hired Hands. Baltimore: University Park Press.

Werner, E. (1990). "High-Risk Children in Young Adulthood: A Longitudinal Study From of Reading. Longman. 423-52.

Whitley, B. E., and Frieze, I. H. (1985). "Children's Causal Attributions for Success and Failure in Achievement Settings: A Meta-Analysis." Journal of Educational Psychology, 81, 131-142.

Word, E.; Achilles, C. M.; Bain, H. P.; Folger, J.; Johnston, J.; and Lentz, M. N. (1990) The State of Tennessee's Student/Teacher Achievement Ratio (STAR) Project: Technical Report. Nashville: Tennessee State Department of Education.